Strengthening Communities

For Titch

Other CDF titles by Steve Skinner

Building Community Strengths (1997)
Assessing Community Strengths (2002) by Steve Skinner and Mandy Wilson

Strengthening communities

A guide to capacity building for communities and the public sector

By Steve Skinner

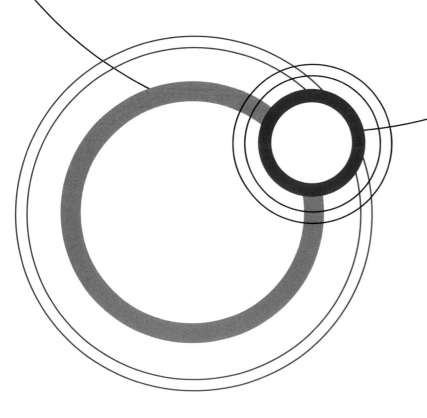

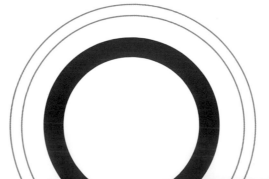

community development foundation

First Published in Great Britain in 2006 by the
Community Development Foundation
Unit 5, Angel Gate
320–326 City Road
London EC1V 2PT
Registered charity number 306130

British Library Cataloguing-in-Publication Data
A record of this publication is available from the British Library.

ISBN 1 901974 68 5

Typesetting by Third Column, Twickenham
Printed in Great Britain by Crowes of Norwich

Contents

Diagrams

Foreword

The current environment of community-oriented policies provides both an enormous challenge and enormous opportunities to those of us working to strengthen communities across Britain.

The ability of the voluntary and community sectors to build the capacity of local communities will be vital in the successful delivery of these policies, but also of crucial importance is the role of the public sector. The modernising agenda in local government, and the introduction of Local Area Agreements place much more emphasis on locally tailored delivery of services, partnership working and effective community engagement.

This book provides not only the background to current policy and the context for capacity building but also a key framework for planners and practitioners. It includes frameworks, practical guidelines and examples from across Britain which help liven the link between theory and practice.

CDF is delighted to publish this book. *Strengthening Communities* should add to the growing awareness of community and agency capacity building as key requirements and challenges, and provide an invaluable resource for all stakeholders working on capacity building theory and practice.

Gabriel Chanan and Alice Wilcock
Policy Directors, Community Development Foundation

Acknowledgements

The author wishes to thank the following people and organisations for their contribution of ideas, information and examples for this publication:

The Active Communities Unit and the Civil Renewal Unit, Home Office
The Community Capacity Building Review Team, Home Office
Neighbourhood Renewal Unit, the Office of the Deputy Prime Minister
The Government Office for Yorkshire and the Humber
Yorkshire and the Humber Regional Forum
The Community Development Foundation
The Community Development Exchange
The Community Work Training Company
COGS – Community Organisations: Growth and Support
Labyrinth Consultancy, Bradford
The Federation of Community Development Learning
The Urban Forum
The University of Bradford Department of Peace Studies and Centre for Community Collaboration
The Building Communities Partnership, Bradford
The Active Citizens Working Group, Bradford
The Community Network, Bradford
The Leeds Multiple Sclerosis Self Help Action Group
The City of Bradford Metropolitan District Council
Blyth Valley Borough Council
The University of Huddersfield, office for Widening Participation
The Housing Association Charitable Trust
The Kendray Initiative, Barnsley
The Burngreave New Deal for Communities Partnership, Sheffield
The Stockwell Partnership, London
The Sandwell Partnership, West Midlands
Regional Action West Midlands

Thanks to: Liz Mabley, Jill Bedford, Sue Gorbing, John Routledge, Peter Taylor, Bev Morton, Steve Hume, Chris Simpson, Amanda Inverarity, Georgina Webster, David Raynor, Mark Hitchen, Charles Woodd, Duncan Prime, John Houghton, Tricia Zipfel, Steve Nesbit, Mervyn Ashby, Loraine Coates, Kevin Ward, Colin Western, Peter Richardson, Sue Shaw, Colin Miller, Jenny Fisher, Linda Mitchell, Margaret Bolton, Tony Herrman, David Evans, Peter Richardson, Pam Hardisty, Kate Faulkes, Sue Faxon, Steve Kingston, Sue Gledhill, Pat Fairfax, Ian Fiddler, Corine Campbell, David Melling, Mick Charlton, Titch Kavanagh, Katherine Wyatt, Pete Browning, John Clark, Daniel Morris, Steve Webster, Sylvia Gibbs, and Andrew Van Doorn.

Particular thanks to the following for the additional time, support or material they gave: Gill Wood, Alan Anderton, Brian Batson, Lee Ling, Mandy Wilson and Pete Wilde; Balraj Sandhu from the Active Communities Unit, the Home Office; Catriona May and Gabriel Chanan from the Community Development Foundation; Professor Jenny Pearce from the Peace Studies Department, University of Bradford for comments on active citizenship; Liz Richardson, formerly at the London School of Economics Centre for Analysis of Social Exclusion, for use of the comparative material on forms of learning and the Seven Stages of Developing a Neighbourhood Project.

Chapter Two: Diagram One is based on material written by the author for the Home Office's community capacity building review report and kindly used with their permission.

Chapter Four: The four building blocks approach was developed with help from: Pat Fairfax, formerly in Bradford Council's Community Development Policy Unit; the Building Communities Partnership, Bradford District; Sue Shaw, freelance consultant, Durham; the Community Development Exchange, Sheffield; the Community Work Training Company, West Yorkshire; the Scottish Centre for Community Development, Glasgow.

Chapter Five: The Community Engagement Model was adapted from an original version developed for the Home Office as the Community Engagement Classification Tool by representatives from CDF, Crime Concern and the Neighbourhood Initiatives Foundation and kindly used with their permission.

Thanks to all these people and organisations for their generous help.

Community Development Foundation (CDF)

The Community Development Foundation, set up in 1968, helps communities achieve greater control over the conditions and decisions affecting their lives by:

- **advising government** and other bodies on community involvement, civil renewal and community cohesion, and measures to build strong, active communities and promote community development

- **supporting community work** of all kinds through networks, links with practitioners, collaborative work with partner organisations and management of local projects

- **carrying out research, evaluation and policy analysis** to identify good practice in all aspects of community development and involvement, and disseminating lessons through training, conferences, publications and consultancy.

CDF is a leading authority on community development in the UK and Europe. It is a non-departmental public body supported principally by the Active Community Directorate of the Home Office with substantial backing from local government, charitable trusts and the private sector. The Community Development Foundation is committed to openness in its affairs, apart from where bound by the need for confidentiality.

Community Development Foundation
Unit 5, Angel Gate
320–326 City Road
London EC1V 2PT
Tel: 020 7226 5375
Fax: 020 7704 0313
Email: admin@cdf.org.uk
Website: www.cdf.org.uk

Registered Charity Number 306130

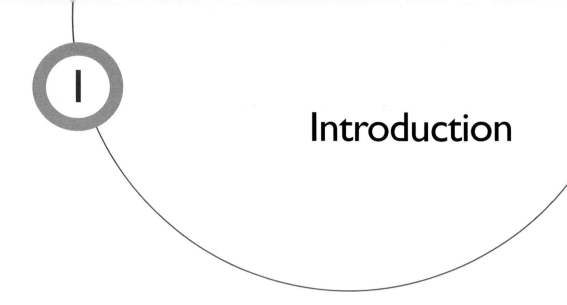

Introduction

Capacity building is about achieving effective community participation and developing strong, well-organised voluntary and community sectors. It's also about the changes needed in public sector organisations so that they can engage more effectively with communities. These two elements of capacity building – growth in communities and changes in agencies – are the main focus of this book. In combination, these lead to the strengthening of communities.

This book is a broad introduction to capacity building, describing a range of approaches, current practice and underlying principles. It provides guidelines, checklists, frameworks and examples from the field, and is based on the experience of many different groups, projects and organisations across Britain.

Building capacity is all about building on and releasing the existing skills, knowledge, experience, confidence and talents that exist in groups and communities. It's about fully valuing what's already there, working in and with communities in ways that empower both people and organisations to grow and develop.

This book has been written in order to create change – to improve practice, to question attitudes and beliefs, to shake up policies and forge new ways of doing things. It can help you to design, plan and provide capacity building activities and programmes and get to grips with what capacity building is all about.

The approach taken in this book

- The book focuses on community groups, rather than larger voluntary sector organisations.

- It looks at capacity building in the context of current government policies and the public sector.

- It provides definitions of key terms.

- It grounds capacity building firmly on key principles and values.

Who is this book for?

It has been written for:

- officers and members of local authorities

- managers, professionals, front-line workers and decision-makers in partnerships and public sector organisations

- civil servants in government offices and departments

- charities and organisations that provide funding and resources for the development of communities

- members of community groups, volunteers and community leaders

- managers and workers in voluntary organisations, regeneration partnerships and development trusts

- colleges and universities interested in community education and engagement

- trainers, community workers, advisors and consultants.

Why was this book written?

The book has been written because:

- new and innovative work on capacity building is being carried out by communities and in the public sector

- many public sector organisations want more information on how to work with communities in supportive roles

- capacity building has become centre stage in a number of key policies

- there is a lack of clarity as to what capacity building is.

Many community workers, groups, networks, consultants and community leaders helped in the creation of this book. In addition, a variety of organisations have contributed material, ideas and comments to this publication (see Acknowledgements). Examples to illustrate points are given from across Britain, as well as particularly drawing on work in the District of Bradford.

What's the need for all this?

Across Britain, many community and voluntary organisations want to increase their effectiveness in achieving their aims and have a bigger role to play in their area. In tandem with this, public sector agencies and local authorities are increasingly interested in engaging with communities, to involve them in the design and delivery of services and work jointly on local initiatives. Consequently, capacity building can be useful both to voluntary and community organisations, and for public sector organisations.

In this publication we define capacity building as:

a process of learning and change that increases the ability of individuals and organisations to contribute to the development of communities.

In other words, capacity building is an approach to developing abilities and organisational effectiveness in any organisation, agency, group, team or project.

- It is a process of learning and change not focused exclusively on communities, though it has often been used with that emphasis in the past.

- The common underlying feature and aim of capacity building in this context, whether in large public sector organisations (we use the shorthand term 'agencies' in this book) or community groups, is that it contributes to the development of communities.

- Capacity building can consequently be seen as a general term that can have additional headings attached to it when referring to particular settings, such as *community capacity building* and in the context of the public sector *agency capacity building*. These terms are explained in Resources One and Two.

What this publication covers

In this publication we look at both *community capacity building* and *agency capacity building*. Broadly speaking, Chapters Two, Three and Four are concerned with community capacity building and Chapter Five focuses on agency capacity building in the context of community engagement.

- Chapter Two explores the role community capacity building can have in a number of policy areas.

- Chapter Three describes the context of the voluntary and community sectors.

- Chapter Four looks more closely at what capacity building in and with communities means in practice.

- Chapter Five discusses capacity building in the public sector where the aim is to enhance community engagement.

- Chapter Six brings the issues together and looks at planning.

This book will steer you through a range of material and ideas drawn from both everyday experience and current policies.

- It is informed by research where possible and aims to be punchy, direct and accessible in style. In places it stirs debate and presents challenges.

- It does not aim to teach practical skills – its aim is more to take an overview and give you an introduction to a number of frameworks and approaches, with references and resources if you want to find out more.

- There is a large resources section in the second half of the book that is more practical or with more detail, based on the issues covered in the first six chapters.

- The standout quotes are either extracts from the main text or based on real life experiences.

Capacity building can be a useful approach for a wide range of different people, partnerships, agencies and organisations. In this book we challenge the assumption that the *main* problem is a lack of capacity in communities and that community groups and leaders should develop their skills and abilities in order to have a seat at the partnership table. Capacity building is *equally* about changes in practices and systems in large public sector bodies, private sector organisations and partnerships.

As a result, this publication directly addresses managers, decision-makers, officers and community practitioners based in partnerships and the public sector.

We all need our capacity built – in the public sector
we need to develop our abilities to work more effectively
and openly with communities

Three main arguments are presented in this book.

● Capacity building with community groups can be organised using four simple themes of Building Skills, Building Organisations, Building Involvement and Building Equality.

● The same four themes can equally be useful to public sector organisations and partnerships in building their capacity for effective community engagement.

● Capacity building needs to be planned and organised in a strategic manner, both at local level and across a whole borough, city or district (we use the term *district* to refer to all of these in this book).

What is the background to all this?

Capacity building as a term has a long history. It was used widely in the mid-1980s in Britain as an imported concept from the United States. Since the late 1980s, capacity building has increasingly been used as an aspect of overseas aid programmes (Eade, 1997). In many Developing World countries, this has focused both on the work of non-governmental organisations as well as at local level. Capacity building in Britain continued through the 1990s to be largely based in regeneration and economic development. Now in the new century, capacity building is taking centre stage – it is much more focused on the voluntary and community sectors, through initiatives such as *Change Up* and *Firm Foundations* as introduced in the box opposite. It also now has a broader central government policy basis underlying it, spanning areas such as civil renewal, active communities and neighbourhood renewal.

What is community capacity building?

As stated, this publication takes the view that capacity building is a general term about learning and change that can be applied to different contexts and settings. The emphasis in this book is on community groups and their networks, and people who are active in their communities. In this context community capacity building can be defined as:

activities, resources and support that strengthen the skills, abilities and confidence of people and community groups to take effective action and leading roles in the development of communities.

There is a need to understand what community capacity building means and what role it can play. The main outcome is that it can support community groups and voluntary organisations to achieve their objectives – this is the underlying inspiration for this book. In addition, it has a role to play in a wide range of policy areas, and we look at this in Chapter Two.

Firm Foundations and Change Up

Firm Foundations

In December 2004 the Home Office launched 'Firm Foundations', the Government's framework for community capacity building. This arose from a review of government support for community capacity building that led to extensive national consultations that informed the final report. Firm Foundations identifies six underlying principles and puts forward four main priority areas for Government action to bring about change. It places community capacity building at the heart of a major high profile Government policy initiative on civil renewal. Civil renewal is presented as dependent on local people having the skills and opportunities to contribute to their communities, engage with civic institutions and influence services that affect their lives. Firm Foundations is discussed more in Chapter Three.

Change Up

The role of larger voluntary and community organisations is changing and increasingly they are involved in taking on the delivery of services. This is partly driven by an increase in the use of commissioning by local authorities and agencies as an alternative to grant aid. In 2002 the Treasury published a cross-cutting review of the role of the voluntary and community sectors in service provision. This key report identified many of the blocks the sectors are facing. Following this, the new national strategy 'Change Up' was launched by the Home Office in 2004. It is designed to build a more effective infrastructure to support the voluntary and community sectors. Change Up is discussed more in Chapter Six.

Questions and answers

It's high time that many questions and myths about capacity building were sorted out.

Isn't capacity building just about support for voluntary and community groups? No, it's also about active citizens, about community leadership, about partnerships and in particular about large agencies changing to achieve effective engagement.

Isn't it rather patronising towards members of community groups? It is unfortunate that as a term *capacity building* sounds patronising. However, it is the term being widely used across the country so the issue is how it is interpreted. This book promotes the use of the term *building strengths* as an alternative to the term *building capacity*. The important thing, whatever it is called, is how it is organised in practice.

Isn't this rather top down? Capacity building should not be forced on people – capacity building should only be organised with support and consensus from participating groups, individuals and organisations. It's about *working with*, not imposing from above. In many cases, it will be led by community groups and networks. In particular it's about supporting groups to achieve their own aims, not just those of external agencies and government.

Haven't we been doing this for years already? Yes, many people working with communities, paid and unpaid, have been involved in initiatives to increase community strengths. The difference now is that, as a recognised field of activity, it can be properly planned and better resourced.

But isn't it just community development with a new title? No, capacity building is not a substitute for community development. It is a part of community development and needs to be based on community development values and principles. In Resource Six we look at what community development work means.

Isn't capacity building just the same thing as empowerment? We argue there is a difference and that empowerment needs to be defined more clearly. Empowerment is essential as the underlying approach to building strengths in communities. This is explored in Chapter Four.

Isn't this all a diversion from the real issue of power and resources? In other words, rather than tackling deprivation, inequality and discrimination, capacity building distracts attention on to the learning agenda and presents the need for change as being only at the grass roots. In practice, it is not an either/or choice – it means tackling both. Building strengths at the grass roots can support initiatives that challenge inequality and discrimination.

The Story

Each chapter ends with The Story, a fictional account of two people – Dave and Gita – going through changes that highlight some of the issues raised in the main text.

Dave used to be an active sort of bloke – football on Sundays, secretary of the social club and a star at pub quizzes – all on top of a day job as a graphic designer. His illness had put a stop to all that – multiple sclerosis was a stressful experience. From being 'able bodied', he'd changed over 18 months to being classed as 'disabled' with a lot of fuss, bother and patronising attitudes from people.

It was a Wednesday – a big day he had to admit – as it meant he was actually going to a group meeting with other people who had MS. It would be his first group since leaving the darts club and the social club – and, yes, it meant really accepting what was going on with his MS. He was now using walking sticks some of the time for getting around and the initial spell of his own cheerful jokes was wearing thin. Getting to the group's new centre was OK – they had paid for a taxi for him and he felt welcomed. Other than that it was all pretty weird – hearing about other people's experiences with so many similarities to his own, sort of depressing and inspiring all in one.

Well, at least he'd made friends with Jimmy, a real fighter, an activist people called him – he was really good fun. 'We'll turn this place into a centre for real changes' he said. 'I've written to some posh bureaucrat in Social Services – Gita Patel – and she's coming here next month. Honestly Dave, she won't know what's hit her.' Jimmy was what really made it for Dave, a real friend. And he'd been invited next week to join the 'MS Assertiveness Group' – sounded all very grand, but Jimmy was in it so it should be OK. Why don't they just call it confidence building? And he could sure do with some of that ...

2 The policy background
– the role of community capacity building

So what are the benefits that arise from community capacity building? What will all this increased capacity actually do? In Chapter Two, we examine how communities and a wide range of organisations, partnerships and agencies as well as central and local government will benefit from enhanced community capacity. This forms the background for the planning and practice of capacity building.

Introduction

Community capacity building has potential to impact on a range of policy areas, such as:

- effective public services
- sustainability, regeneration and enterprise
- civil renewal
- community cohesion
- strong communities.

There is obviously overlap between these broad headings; these are particular examples rather than describing the total range of impact. The role of community capacity building in these policy areas is shown visually in Diagram 1 below. Understanding the role that community capacity building has to play is important so that the voluntary and community sectors, government departments, local authorities and agencies can identify the contribution it makes.

A key focus of this book is on the community groups. Consequently the following discussion on the policy role of capacity building focuses on *community capacity building*. Each of the examples of policy impact is now looked at in turn.

Effective public services

The modernisation of public services is now a key concern for agencies and central and local government. Local authorities are under pressure from public and government agencies such as the Audit Commission and the National Audit Office to improve services. The Office of the Deputy Prime Minister has set out an ambitious ten-year vision for local government, including the modernisation of public services (ODPM, 2004a). Public sector organisations often have demanding targets to achieve,

Review of government departments

In 2003 the Home Office carried out research to find out how government departments viewed capacity building. This was a part of the work of the review of government support for community capacity building. One of the key findings of the review was that there is a lack of recognition of the vital role that capacity building in communities plays in supporting a wide range of policy goals. It showed that while there is a high level of commitment to community involvement in many departments, there was little understanding of *why* it is important or that to be effective it requires planning and resourcing.

Source: *Building Civil Renewal*, Home Office, 2004a

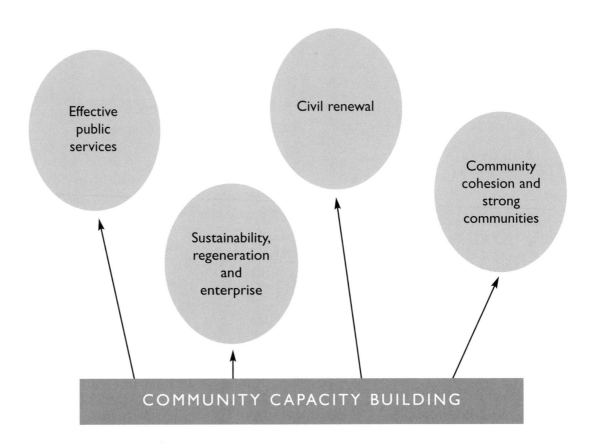

Diagram 1: *Examples of the role of community capacity building in policy areas*

linked, for example, to the *Children Act* 2004 and NHS reforms. Local area agreements, currently at pilot stage in a limited number of areas, have improved services as their prime concern.

So how can community capacity building contribute to more effective services? To understand this, it is useful first to look at the wider role of both the voluntary and community sectors. HM Treasury's cross-cutting review of the role of the voluntary and community sectors in service delivery was published in 2002, and recognised several areas of added value that both voluntary and community organisations bring to service delivery. These are (HM Treasury, 2002, p. 16):

● specialist knowledge, experience and skills

● delivery of more personalised services closer to users' needs

- particular ways of involving people in service delivery, both as users and as providers of self help

- independence from public sector service provision

- access to the wider community without institutional baggage

- freedom and flexibility from institutional pressures.

Identifying these qualities has helped to support the increased role of both the voluntary and community sectors in providing services, expressed through the Change Up initiative. Further discussion of the role of the voluntary and community sectors (VCS) in supporting services is given in a key central government report published in 2005 (HM Treasury, 2005). The focus of this Chapter is with the *community sector*: Key points concern the roles of the community sector in providing and enhancing services:

Formal services

It needs to be recognised that many community organisations and groups deliver formal services, though often on a small, locally-based scale. They span a wide range of public issues and services, including, for example, health, employment, education and housing.

Informal services

The services and resources provided by the community sector include a significant level of informal volunteering, informal advice and advocacy and networks of support within neighbourhoods and communities. This in combination can be described as *social capital*, a term discussed below, p16. In other words, self-help and mutual aid can be seen as a form of service and a resource that contributes to the quality of life.

Contribution to design of services

In terms of contributing to decision-making on local services, community groups will often have specialist knowledge and expertise, for example, where tenants' organisations are taking lead roles in the management of local authority housing. In some policy areas, community groups may not have specialist technical knowledge but may contribute in depth knowledge of the local area and its problems.

The spread of community organisations' work on public issues

Public issues	Example of relevant community organisations
Employment	Groups providing training
Health	Sports clubs Food co-ops
Education	After school clubs Community centres
Housing	Tenants' groups
Environment	Residents' associations

Adapted from *Regeneration and Sustainable Communities* (Chanan, West, Garratt and Humm, 1999)

Access to marginalised groups

Some community organisations, such as community-run community centres, provide a wide range of both informal and formal services to their local communities and neighbourhoods, often providing greater access to marginalised groups than statutory agencies or larger voluntary organisations could achieve.

In aggregate, given its size, the whole local community sector can be seen to deliver a significant level of services. The community sector is highly productive but hard to assess in its contribution to the overall volume of services because it is partly outside the monetary system and often not recognised by the public sector. A definition of 'community sector' is discussed in Chapter Three.

Policy outcomes

To sum up, increased capacity in the community sector can contribute to more effective services in the following ways:

- **increased quality and flexibility of local services** – involving community groups in delivering services will increase diversity of provision that can address the needs of different communities, through delivering formal and in particular informal services.

- **increased access to local services** – by creating new channels to contact and engage with hard to reach and minority service users.

- **increased level of accountability of services** – through more effective and broader-based participation in planning and improvement.

Community capacity building and local authorities

For local authorities, the Office of the Deputy Prime Minister's ten-year vision has prompted increased focus on citizen engagement and participation. It proposes that the role of local government is changing from primarily service delivery to accountable leadership for the whole community. *The Future of Local Government*, published by ODPM in 2004, argues that a high level of engagement is needed to build social capital and civic life. It is also needed to ensure public services are more effective in meeting needs. Following this, in early 2005 ODPM brought out two publications for consultation.

- *Why Neighbourhoods Matter* promotes a new framework for neighbourhoods advocating the view that there should be opportunities for a neighbourhood arrangement everywhere (ODPM, 2005a). With no 'one size fits all' solution, a range of options is explored including neighbourhood charters. What is important is that *Why Neighbourhoods Matter* recognises that capacity building will be needed at local level for this to happen (ODPM, 2005a).

- The second publication, *Vibrant Local Leadership*, takes these ideas further, suggesting that councillors can have a key and unique role to play in neighbourhood involvement. As leaders, councillors can facilitate sections of the community to organise and have a voice in local issues (ODPM 2005b).

This prompts the question: how are councillors supported to do this? Many councillors will quite rightly be requesting support in the development of their roles. It also raises wider questions about the nature of community representation and involvement. These are discussed in Resource Three.

Local area agreements

Local area agreements (LAAs) can create effective links between service improvements and capacity building.

LAAs were established on a pilot basis in 2004 with 21 selected areas identified later that year. The aims of LAAs are to 'improve both the effectiveness and the efficiency of the way in which government works with local authorities and their delivery partners' (ODPM, 2004b, p. 3). The idea of a local agreement is that it will simplify dealings with central government by allowing greater co-ordination between and flexibility in the use of funding streams. LAAs are based on three themes or blocks, which are Children and Young People, Safer and Stronger Communities, and Healthier and Older People.

LAAs have a number of advantages. They will:

- focus on a range of agreed outcomes that are shared by all the delivery partners locally

- simplify the number of additional funding streams from central government going into an area, help to join up public services more effectively and allow greater flexibility for local solutions for particular local circumstances

- help devolve decision-making, moving away from a 'Whitehall knows best' philosophy and reducing bureaucracy (ODPM, 2004c).

From the perspective of community capacity building, LAAs do present some new opportunities for public sector organisations and particularly local authorities to take a fresh look at their relationship with the VCS. Advice Note One specifically requests the involvement of the VCS in 'helping to identify, shape and deliver local services. The LAA should include a statement on how it builds on the infrastructure or capacity building services developed through Change Up, where relevant, and the capacity building support provided through Firm Foundations' (ODPM, 2004b, p. 5).

This guidance is helpful to promote the role that community capacity building has to play in LAAs. Within the block 'Safer and Stronger Communities', a mandatory outcome is:

'To empower local people to have a greater voice and influence over local decision-making and the delivery of services.'

(ODPM, 2004b, p. 17)

This is a useful starting position that is to be welcomed, and presents opportunities for a central voluntary and community sector role and the support of capacity building. It does perhaps need to be expanded and strengthened – as an outcome, its focus is on influence rather than the other broader options for engagement such as service delivery and joint working. Equally, if the LAA is to include a statement on community capacity building, it would be useful for that to include an outcome. No doubt the pilots will examine these issues and produce constructive ways to address them.

Sustainability, regeneration and enterprise

Urban regeneration policy over the last two decades has increasingly recognised the value of community participation and community capacity at project, programme and partnerships levels. Interest by government in participation culminated in the national strategy for neighbourhood renewal. The National Strategy for Neighbourhood Renewal committed the Government to making sure that communities' needs and priorities are in the foreground in neighbourhood renewal and that residents of poor neighbourhoods are given the tools to get involved in whatever way they want. This major initiative instigated a new approach to regeneration, with less focus on area-based, time-limited programmes. The neighbourhood renewal strategy, as well as containing other key features, emphasised that effective local leadership and community participation will help to bring improvements in mainstream services and the quality of life across neighbourhoods and communities. The Community Participation Programme has been an integral part of this, containing funds designed to enhance the involvement of communities in regeneration. The panel below describes the aims for community participation underlying this scheme.

Central government policy on participation

The Office of the Deputy Prime Minister (ODPM) published the Single Community Programme guidance in November 2003 (ODPM, 2003a). This gave greater clarity to the ODPM's aims for community participation and contained four high level goals. Their guidance states:

'These high-level goals should inform all aspects of neighbourhood renewal and provide a clear focus for the Single Community Programme (CP). They are in line with the thrust of policy developments in the ODPM, Home Office and Government more widely.'

(ODPM, 2003a, p. 5)

- **Social capital** – CP aims to increase the confidence and capacity of individuals and small groups to get involved in activities that improve their quality of life and build mutually supportive relationships that enhance neighbourliness and hold communities together.

- **Social inclusion and cohesion** – CP aims to develop empowered communities, able to tackle complex problems, including negative attitudes and values, capable of developing a common vision, a sense of belonging, a positive identity where diversity is valued and celebrated, and a community that has positive external networks as well as internal cohesion.

- **Service delivery** – CP aims to ensure that local communities are in a position to influence service delivery and the use of resources, by helping define problems, set priorities, develop and deliver solutions, to strengthen their ability to take responsibility for their neighbourhoods, and build professional and institutional capacity to plan and deliver community-based/community-led solutions where appropriate.

- **Governance** – CP aims to enable people to exercise the right to participate in decisions that affect the wellbeing of their communities, to support the development of a 'community voice' at many levels, to build community networks, to enable communities to participate as equal partners, and to increase accountability between local communities, service providers and other decision-makers.

The on-going challenge now is to transfer them to the context of the Safer and Stronger Communities Fund and local area agreements.

Another key policy initiative with implications for community capacity building is the Government's Communities Plan *Sustainable Communities: Building for the Future* which was launched in 2003 (ODPM, 2003b). The Plan sets out a long-term programme of action for delivering sustainable communities in both urban and rural areas. The Plan covers initiatives to tackle housing shortage, improving the local environment and protecting the countryside. Effective engagement and participation by local people and groups, especially in the planning, design and long-term stewardship of their community, is seen by Government as a central feature of sustainability. Community capacity building will consequently play a key role in sustainability initiatives such as Building for the Future.

Enterprise

Community capacity building provides major opportunities to increase employability and enterprise in individuals and groups who may not easily access other available gateways to training and support.

● Community capacity building can involve a wide range of forms of adult learning, such as mentoring, that improves skills and knowledge in an accessible way for non-traditional learners.

● The skills involved, for example, in local residents managing a community building, in parents running a child care group or volunteering to help organise a play scheme, are directly transferable to the jobs market.

These overlaps between the community capacity building and enterprise are increasingly being recognised by funders and policy makers. For example, the policies underlying the community economic development priority within the European structural funds have recognised the close link between community capacity and economic capacity, strengthened by an influential report produced in 1996 (Lloyd, 1996). The criteria for European structural funds in programmes such as Objective One and Two have also, through particular Priorities, increasingly valued the role of community participation and the need to build an underlying base of community capacity.

The Framework for Community Economic Development

This useful framework was developed in the South Yorkshire Objective One area as a means of gauging community capacity in the context of economic development. It suggests five levels of capacity, described as communities:

● with low level of co-ordinated community activity and resources

● with some established groups, some newly emerging and developing infrastructure

● with a range of community activities and some formal networks and infrastructure in place

● that are active, well organised and involved in community economic development

● with a track record of community economic development and effective partnership working.

This framework was further developed for a method called Assessing Community Strengths, see Chapter Six.

Policy outcomes

To summarise, in the context of enterprise, regeneration and sustainability, it can be argued that enhanced community capacity will contribute to a range of government policy objectives, for example:

Enterprise: Community organisations can provide skills and organisational structures that can support community enterprise.

Adult learning progression: Participation in community-based learning can increase access to further learning for marginalised groups.

Employment: Involvement in community initiatives, projects, groups and networks can develop transferable skills.

Sustainability: Enhancing local leadership skills and building the community management of projects and assets can contribute to sustainable regeneration.

Economic capacity building

Capacity building can be seen as a generic process of individual learning and organisational development that can be applied to different sectors. For example, *economic capacity building* is where the intended outcomes are to do with increased wealth and employment. This may mean creating environments where economic activity is supported, and vocational skills are developed. Economic capacity building is a phrase developed by Oxfam referring to a range of support that increases people's abilities to generate and earn income collectively and improve their conditions and security. It often involves practical assistance and training for micro-enterprises, co-operatives and small businesses as well as improving financial and trade arrangements. As well as collective involvement, it could include capacity building for increased employability; much European funding through ERDF and ESF programmes has been directed to forms of vocational training called capacity building. This consequently would be better termed economic capacity building to separate it from community capacity building, which is less concerned with individual benefit as the main outcome (Eade, 1997).

Civil renewal

Civil renewal is a policy initiative launched by the Home Office in 2003. Underlying civil renewal is a concern that in British society, democratic institutions are losing community support. The perception is that due to current cultural and technological trends, people are losing their 'civic values' (Home Office, 2003a). The causes identified include:

- increased mobility
- the decline of workplace-based social support
- the growth of 'instant satisfaction' consumerism.

Certainly there are trends to worry about – in particular electoral participation in 2001 at a turnout of 59.4% was the lowest since 1918, having fallen from 72% in 1992. Consequently a key part of the agenda for civil renewal is to address the decline in the level of electoral participation, which is called the 'democratic deficit'. Two key terms used in the civil renewal agenda – *active citizenship* and *social capital* – are looked at in the boxes opposite and on page 16.

In practice, civil renewal comes down to three specific areas of government support. Broadly these cover:

- **Individuals** – enhancing active citizenship: giving people more opportunities to tackle community problems

- **Groups** – strengthening community organisations: collective action to deal with common concerns

- **Partnerships** – building public sector and area-based partnerships' abilities to involve citizens and communities more effectively in the planning and delivery of services.

Given that community capacity building spans all three of these themes, it has a significant potential in enhancing civil renewal. Community capacity building works through many pathways:

- with *people* to help build skills and confidence through collective activity

- with *groups and networks* to help make them more effective, inclusive and empowering

- it will also strengthen *partnerships*, in supporting more accountable and skilful community representation.

Key concepts

Active citizenship

Active citizenship is being promoted by the Home Office as part of its civil renewal agenda. A key aspect of active citizenship, from the Government's point of view, is that it combines involvement in democracy and social inclusion. It addresses a concern that some citizens may become increasingly alienated from the decision-making processes in terms of policies and services – the concept of active citizenship helps to build bridges between community participation and local governance.

Useful points concerning the nature of active citizenship are:

- Active citizenship can be understood to involve both *behaviours* such as voluntary activity, voting or acting as a representative as well as *attitudes* that help to sustain communities and inhibit anti-social behaviour (Whiteley, 2004).

- Active citizenship can include both individualistic and collective forms of participation.

The emphasis of this book is on the latter.

Active citizenship can have a range of benefits for different stakeholders:

- **the individual** who is active may benefit from new skills, social contacts, a sense of value and achievement

- **the group** they join may gain practical help and support

- **the public sector agency** may benefit through improved design of services and greater legitimacy in the area

- **the local authority** may benefit from increased democratic participation

- **the state** may benefit, in policy terms, through improved governance and increased civil renewal, inclusion and social capital.

Policy outcomes

In the context of civil renewal, enhanced community capacity can potentially contribute to a range of public and government policy objectives, for example:

- **Governance:** Increased connection with democratic structures and participation in civic life

- **Citizenship learning:** Increased participation in citizenship learning, especially by excluded groups and non-traditional learners

- **Social capital:** Help to create and maintain healthy, connected communities through strengthening grass-roots informal networking and organisation.

Further research is needed to understand more fully the causal relationships in these areas and the Home Office is funding a research programme to address this.

Key concepts

Social capital

The concept of social capital has now become a key policy concern of central government. It is about shared understandings, levels of trust, associational memberships and informal networks that help social exchange and social order and underpin social institutions. In particular in involves building 'bonds' and 'bridges' between people to provide a platform for social support and community relationships. In terms of the link between social capital and civil renewal, the assumption is that enhanced social capital will act as part of the foundations for more effective governance (HM Treasury, 2005). This can be understood through seeing community involvement as having two distinct dimensions:

- **horizontal involvement** – involvement in community activity, such as being a member of a friendship network, a club, community group or neighbourhood organisation. This is where individuals are involved in local community activity, informal volunteering, forming new groups, involvement in social networks, self-help and community action that builds social capital and trust.

- **vertical involvement** – involvement in governance, such as voting, influencing local decision-making or representing a community interest in a partnership. It also includes involvement in, for example, the local management of community centres, projects, initiatives and programmes.

Horizontal and vertical involvement are distinctive areas (Chanan, 2002). Horizontal involvement can be seen as a key part of social capital. The assumption is that increased horizontal involvement in a community will strengthen the vertical involvement in governance. However, what is not clear from the available literature is that while there is clear evidence of a decline in political participation in Britain over the last two decades, there is not such clarity concerning the presumed decline in social capital.

> ## Rural areas
>
> In rural areas, the Government has been increasingly interested in community participation as a way to solve problems. The Rural White Paper in 2000 set out a new vision for villages and rural areas, emphasising the key role to be played by local groups and communities. The 'Vital Villages' programme, initiated by the Countryside Agency, aims to achieve 'empowered, active and inclusive communities' (Ellis et al 2004, p. 3). DEFRA's plan for supporting rural community capacity building is about everyone playing an active part by providing support for local volunteering, social capital, community action and voluntary sector running of services in rural areas in England (Barton, 2003).

Community cohesion

The disturbances in several cities in 2001 led to a new initiative nationally to increase community cohesion. A new Community Cohesion Unit was established in central government and the 88 local authority areas receiving neighbourhood renewal funding were required to produce community cohesion strategies by 2003. The Denham Report (Denham, 2001) provided important insights and recommendations into the causes and solutions of the disturbances and broadened the agenda. The concept of community cohesion has been developed since then into a much wider perspective, where in addition to focusing on relationships based on ethnicity, other issues are being included, for example, gender, sexuality and disability (Local Government Association, 2004). Many projects and groups are interested and motivated to contribute to community cohesion but unsure how to address the issues in a sensitive and constructive manner. Community capacity building can help to address this need through developing skills, knowledge and confidence, especially of marginalised people and through supporting increased contact and communication between groups of different identities and backgrounds. However, addressing cohesion issues through capacity building in communities needs to avoid superficiality. Capacity building activities and programmes will need to be organised carefully to consider issues of equality and diversity if they are not in some cases done in ways that empower already dominant groups (discussed in Chapter Four, pp. 55ff). More fundamentally, progress towards greater cohesion in communities will be limited without addressing underlying inequalities in the distribution of opportunities, resources and influence (Gilchrist, 2004).

Policy outcomes

While bearing these issues in mind, increased capacity at community level could contribute to community cohesion in the following ways.

- **Inclusion:** Capacity building can strengthen the level of community organisation of excluded groups. This will enable increased active participation by such groups in mainstream society, for example, as both users and providers of services.

- **Diversity:** Community-based learning can be an arena for increased cultural understanding between groups and communities of different backgrounds. It can be an opportunity for groups to learn about each other and to learn together.

- **Leadership:** Increased confidence and skills can be developed through community activity, and networking can increase active citizenship and contribute to building effective community leadership in marginalised groups.

- **Resolving conflicts** – These are important skills to develop in groups and community leaders, helping resolve conflicts and tensions at an early stage.

Strong communities

If capacities are built and communities are strengthened, what would this look like? What would it lead to, both in communities and for the public sector? These are complex questions and only a start can be given here to answering them, drawing on current research and practice.

To recap on the definition of *community capacity building*:

> *Activities, resources and support that strengthen the skills, abilities and confidence of people and community groups to take effective action and leading roles in the development of communities.*

This means communities showing increased capacity would have:

- **People:** volunteers, community representatives, active residents, leaders and community entrepreneurs who are confident, well informed, skilful and effective.

- **Groups:** groups, voluntary organisations, networks and communities of interest that are well organised, secure and properly resourced, that address diverse needs, resolve conflicts, support members and serve their communities.

In summary, capacity building in and with communities will enhance and release the abilities of *people and groups* to help others, relate to others of different backgrounds, take part, organise, manage, work collectively, be enterprising, resolve conflicts, represent, contribute to decision making, and act on the basis of fairness.

If this process is about strengthening communities, then it leads to the question of what a *strong community* would look like. Given that the term *strong* or *stronger communities* is now being widely used, a definition would be useful We. provide a working definition – one put forward as a draft that can be debated and developed.

Working definition of a strong community

A strong community is active, organised, participative, accepting, connected and fair.

- **Active** – people are active in tackling community problems and improving the quality of life.

- **Organised** – people come together to form and sustain organisations that deal with common problems and provide effective and accessible services.

- **Participative** – people and groups contribute to decisions that affect their lives, contribute to civic life and the governance of institutions and services.

- **Accepting** – people are accepting of each other, with an understanding of different cultures, traditions and beliefs, with the diversity of backgrounds and circumstances being positively valued.

- **Connected** – there is a sense of belonging; people and groups from different backgrounds have contact and communication and, where appropriate, there is joint working between groups.

- **Fair** – people from different backgrounds and identities have similar life opportunities with equal access to services, employment and resources; groups are actively tackling exclusion and discrimination.

This working definition draws on Government policy on neighbourhood renewal, community cohesion and civil renewal, as well as the Government's Guidance on local area agreements. It is also partly based on the definition of community cohesion published by the Local Government Association (LGA, 2004).

A number of questions arise from this definition.

- **What does it mean?** It describes an end state – in other words, it presents the general outcome of increased capacity at community level. An end state means a condition that we can work towards in terms of planning support for communities, not just in capacity building but in a range of ways. Some neighbourhoods may already display a high level of these qualities while others may have a low starting point. How we achieve progress is the theme of this book.

- **How can it be used?** The definition of a *strong community* will have a number of potential uses in neighbourhoods and district-wide strategies. For example, it could be used as part of a community strategy or strategic plan on community capacity building. For local area agreements, this definition may inform and support the contribution of the voluntary and community sectors.

- **How can it be developed?** This definition is just an outline – each district may wish to develop its own vision of being 'stronger'. For this reason the description is kept short and general, to be developed further as needed. Whatever adaptations are made, the underlying principles contained within the definition will need to be kept.

- **What support would it need?** A *strong community* will need partnerships, public and private sector organisations to look at themselves to assess how much they are supporting these qualities. A strong community would need institutions and services that mirror these qualities in their policies and practices. Community engagement forms a vehicle for how this can be developed – we discuss this in Chapter Five.

- **What principles underlie it?** A *strong community* is a fair one where community participation, through different channels and organisations, is open to everyone in the locality. Within the broad spread of voluntary and community sectors and their range of groups and support, a strong community would not be a place where some groups are excluded because of, for example, their age, beliefs or cultural background. We discuss this further in Chapter Four, pages 55ff.

- **How do we achieve it?** A whole variety of processes, support and community development work would be involved, based both in communities and in agencies. Capacity building is only a part of such a range, not by any means the only or main contributor to this.

- **What is the link with community cohesion?** The definition of a *strong community* given here includes implicit reference to community cohesion. In other words, completely integral to the concept of being *stronger* are the principles underlying community cohesion. These are reflected in the three features of a strong community as being accepting, connected and fair. This integration means that the policy within *Safer and Stronger Communities* would reflect the cohesion agenda if it used this definition of strong communities (ODPM and Home Office, 2004).

- **How can it be measured?** How we measure progress and evaluate effectiveness in building stronger communities is crucial. Further discussion of this appears in Resource Eight.

Conclusions

From this brief review of the role of community capacity building we can make the following general observations:

● Community capacity building has the potential to have a major impact on a range of key policy and service areas, benefiting central government, agencies, local government and local communities.

● For local authorities, it has the potential to contribute positively to a wide range of policy areas that are central to current priorities.

● Further research is needed to identify more precisely the causal link between different forms of community capacity building and specific policy outcomes.

Having described the role of community capacity building in terms of key policies and services, we move on in the next Chapter to look at the nature of the voluntary and community sectors.

The Story

It was a Friday afternoon and Gita felt tense. This was her first week in her new job – with a grand title of 'Senior Manager for Commissioning Services'. A strong coffee was helping. She had moved up quickly through the ranks of the Council, having a family background in business – she'd started in her dad's shop as a twelve-year-old and had developed some pretty hard business skills along the way. Friday, at least, was office day, and that meant a chance to catch up on the avalanche of emails …

There were two that had caught her eye, mainly because she knew little about either. Her Director had written – in friendly terms – asking her to prepare a paper on how voluntary groups that the department worked with could be 'integrated more into the mainstream agenda' – she hated the jargon. The note included something on 'identifying capacity building needs' – another obscure term, no doubt the latest fashion he had picked up at some expensive conference.

The second email that caught her eye was directly from a group who sounded interesting – at least as they were giving her an invitation to something. Would she go to meet the Multiple Sclerosis Action Group at their new centre? This sounded a bit more like it, a trip out from the office, with tea and cakes and a nice chat. To 'discuss enhancing their role in taking on service delivery' – yes that had potential. So next month, yes that would be a bit more like it. Meanwhile there's that budget to sort out and tomorrow's planning meeting to prepare for and …

The context
– understanding the voluntary and community sectors

Chapter Three gives an outline of the voluntary and community sectors, arguing that there is a need to recognise the community sector has a particular set of roles. We also look at communities of interest, networks, active citizenship and infrastructure, as they are all part of the context of community capacity building.

Introduction

The main points argued in Chapter Three are that:

- communities of interest and networks as well as community groups need to be considered in planning capacity building

- active citizenship is a useful concept but much wider in scope than the voluntary and community sectors

- the infrastructure of the voluntary and community sectors needs to be based in those sectors, not in the public sector

- partnerships, the public and private sectors as well as further and higher education institutions can also provide useful support for capacity building.

Chapter Three describes the environment within which *community capacity building* takes place. This is important in order to plan capacity building activities and programmes in ways that address needs.

The voluntary and community sectors

The voluntary and community sectors (VCS) are a significant force across the country. The sheer scale of the sectors needs to be recognised in policy making, and they need to be accepted as major partners at local, regional and national levels.

A second key feature is diversity. Across Britain, the voluntary and community sectors include a wide range of organisations, from small self-help groups to large national charities. Some charities are household names, such as Barnardos and Age Concern, employing thousands of staff, with centres across the country. Within the voluntary and community sectors there is a rich diversity of cultures and faith groups.

The scale of the voluntary and community sectors

The number of voluntary organisations and community groups in the UK has been estimated at approximately 150,000 registered charities plus a further 250,000 voluntary and community organisations (HM Treasury, 2005). Bradford District, for example, with a population of nearly half a million, has an estimated 3,500 voluntary and community sector organisations and groups, and Leeds, with a population of approximately two-thirds of a million, up to 5,000. Blyth Valley in the north east has well over 600 active voluntary and community organisations across the borough, with over 5,000 volunteers and over 200 employees. The National Council for Voluntary Organisations estimates that 'general charities' in the UK had a total income of £15 billion in 2000–01. It is estimated that the sectors' contribution to UK GDP was worth over £7 billion per annum in 2001–02 (HM Treasury, 2005).

At regional level, research on the economic value of the voluntary and community sectors, for example those studies carried out in Cornwall and Devon, Yorkshire and the West Midlands, have helped to increase the understanding of their contribution. In Wakefield District volunteers alone contribute between £45–63 million worth of time to the local economy (WYLDA, 2004).

Defining the voluntary and community sectors

The majority of the voluntary organisations and community groups are small in size – one estimate puts this at 80% of the total (NCVO, 2004). These types of groups often have a less formal structure than the larger voluntary sector organisations, have lower or no income and are membership based, and in combination are called the community sector. A useful definition of the community sector adopted by CDF is:

The whole range of autonomous collective and group activity, directly undertaken by individuals within their neighbourhood or community of interest, to improve the quality of life.

The community sector is consequently a spectrum, which includes community groups and similar collective activities as a whole. It relates to a wide range of policies and services including, for example, activities such as playgroups, tenants' associations, arts and sports groups, environmental and leisure groups, scout groups, religious welfare groups, self-help and support groups, community centres and village halls. The community sector can consequently be seen as the community itself taking action to get things done (Home Office, 2003b). Many community sector groups are not funded and some may have no written constitution yet may be providing important informal services, help and support.

The voluntary sector differs from the community sector. A useful definition of the voluntary sector is:

'Organisations whose activities are carried out other than for profit but which are not public or local authorities. These organisations would normally be formally constituted and employ paid professional and administrative staff. They may or may not use volunteer help.'

(Home Office, 2004b, p. 40)

There are two features that help to distinguish between community and voluntary sector groups and organisations:

- **Size:** as described, generally the community sector is made up of small organisations and groups – one definition, for example, suggests any group with less than two staff or equivalent is part of the community sector (Chanan, 2002).

- **Control:** generally community sector groups and organisations are run predominantly by their *individual* users, members or local residents. In contrast, many larger voluntary organisations have management committees made up predominantly of professionals from agencies, representatives or staff from other groups or voluntary organisations, their own staff, members of the council etc.

This is where it gets tricky – there are some examples where a large organisation with a substantial base of resources and staff is clearly run by a board of local residents – in other words it displays a mixture of features of both voluntary and community sector organisations. The Royds Community Association in south Bradford is a good example, which, as a successful regeneration partnership, employs several staff and has a large asset base, yet has clearly been run by local people who have been elected on a regular basis.

The key point is that, in practice, there is no clear dividing line between the voluntary and community sectors. We believe it best to see the two sectors as a continuum, with some overlaps in the middle. Voluntary organisations make a major contribution to delivering services, both under contract from agencies and directly in response to need. Community sector organisations are less likely to be involved in delivering public services in a formal contractual sense. Some deliver public services working in partnership with larger voluntary organisations. Both the voluntary and community sectors between them contribute a huge range of activities, volunteers, representatives and resources to the areas they are working in.

There is no clear dividing line between the
voluntary and community sectors

The community sector

At local level, there is a tremendous amount of involvement of people providing help and support between neighbours or based around schools, clubs, village halls and community centres. People may be active not just as a member of a group but in an informal capacity, often unrecognised but essential for the welfare and stability of our communities. The citizenship survey of 2001 in England and Wales, based on a sample of 15,475 people, showed 67% volunteered informally at least once a year and 34% volunteered informally at least once a month. This is equivalent to 14.2 million people in England and Wales (Home Office, 2001). The data revealed that both formal and informal volunteering had lower levels of participation in areas of deprivation. The citizenship survey also showed that nearly 22 million were involved socially in clubs, groups and organisations at least once a month and of these, 11% were in local community or neighbourhood groups. This indicates the rich layer of activity that exists in neighbourhoods and communities.

Why define them as two sectors?

If there is a continuum between the two sectors, why define them as two sectors at all – why not just call all this community and voluntary activity the 'voluntary sector' or, as proposed by HM Treasury, the term 'third sector' (HM Treasury, 2005)? The reason for not doing this is because the needs of the smaller community groups and their concerns will not be addressed in terms of resources and support. In practice, the development needs of a major charity operating at district level will be different from those for example of a tenants' association. For this reason the Community Sector Coalition was formed nationally to represent and advocate the needs of the community sector. The smaller groups need representation at both local and national level; consequently using both terms *voluntary sector* and *community sector* is important. For example, the Firm Foundations report (Home Office, 2004b), specifically focuses on the needs of community groups. Consequently, in this publication we use and promote the term voluntary and community *sectors*. What is important is that the two sectors are not seen by their members as two divided camps; it needs to be recognised that there is a lot in common between the two sectors and both have a tremendous contribution to make. Representation from both sectors on partnerships and decision-making bodies is best not divided up too obsessively.

Joint working between large and small community and voluntary organisations

Smaller community organisations can get involved in providing services, in some cases by working jointly with larger voluntary organisations. A scoping study, published by the National Council for Voluntary Organisations in 2005, examines the potential for these arrangements. Certainly there are benefits for both large and small organisations; large organisations, such as national charities, may benefit from better information on the communities they are working in and access to an increased range of other providers. It can improve the image of the larger organisation, which is seen as a builder of relationships rather than adopting the 'helicopter in' approach. Small organisations can increase their access to the systems, policies and resources of the larger organisation, and grow in confidence through the relationship. For it to go well it does involve time and resources, especially in the initial phase of joint working. The report concludes that these partnerships demonstrate that the voluntary and community sectors can substantially benefit from collaborative working and use it to strengthen their position in obtaining contracts (NCVO, 2005).

What particular capacity building is needed in the community sector?

Community workers working directly with community groups know from their everyday experience how the needs differ between larger voluntary organisations and community groups. Research carried out by the Centre for Voluntary Action at Aston Business School for the Home Office provides clear evidence that the smaller community organisations have particular needs.

- Small organisations are often heavily dependent on a small number of committed individuals working in a voluntary capacity without the support of professional staff.

- They can suffer from blurred roles, such as a mixture of the strategic and operational, and a lack of clarity between the formal and informal aspect of relationships.

- Small organisations often face particular difficulties in retaining trustees and chairs face specific training needs not met by training aimed at trustees in general.

- Small organisations showed an overemphasis on recruiting trustees with technical expertise rather than valuing overall governance and team-building skills.

The research confirmed the need to provide support on effective governance that reflects the particular circumstances of small organisations (Home Office, 2004a). Community groups in rural areas may have particular characteristics compared with those based in urban areas that can affect their capacity building needs. They may have greater responsibility for providing more local services, and, while being more involved with other groups within their village or parish, can be relatively disconnected from networks outside their area (Home Office, 2004c).

Communities of interest

The understanding of the voluntary and community sectors has changed in the last few years. *Communities of interest* are now recognised as a key part of the VCS and can be defined as:

> *Groups of people who share an identity, for example African Caribbean people, or who share an experience, for example, being homeless and who often face discrimination and barriers to influencing and accessing services, resources and support.*

(Adapted from The Building Communities Partnership, 2004, p. 18)

Communities of interest may be dispersed across a district and come together to work for their rights and achieve greater equality. They are not the same as, but are often confused with, single-issue lobby groups. The phrase 'communities of interest' includes, for example, women, ethnic minorities, gypsy travellers, gay, lesbian and bisexual people and people with disabilities.

A key feature of communities of interest is that they are people who are organised into groups or networks on the basis of shared identity and common experience, rather than where they live. People organise together for a variety of reasons such as:

- to get support from each other

- because they do not feel safe or confident about sharing their perspectives and needs with other people in a local neighbourhood – for example some gay, lesbian and bisexual people feel this

- they will be more strongly organised and better represented by joining together across a whole area or district.

Public sector agencies are increasingly recognising the need to engage with communities of interest. Recognition of communities of interest is especially important where local authorities and agencies are preoccupied with area and neighbourhood-based planning. Many communities of interest do not easily relate to consultation and involvement when organised on a geographical basis. This tendency has marginalised many people who, for a variety of reasons, are in effect excluded from participation. It is ironic that the neighbourhood renewal strategy has in many cases led to a focus on geographically-based issues yet it was established as part of a national policy on social exclusion.

Capacity building will need to consider that communities of interest vary greatly in their level of organisation. Some have district-wide networks, and have their own projects or centres which receive funding and employ staff. Others may be fragmented in a small number of isolated groups or clubs, with little contact with each other or with agencies in any organised manner. Any one person may be part of more than one community of interest as well as being a member of a neighbourhood group. It is important not to label people and assume their whole identity is based on their involvement in any one group.

EXAMPLE

Neighbourhood renewal action planning in Bradford

This example shows how work with communities of interest is being integrated into neighbourhood renewal.

Bradford's innovative approach to neighbourhood renewal has focused on grass-roots involvement in neighbourhood action plans to inform how services are delivered locally. The district now has over 60 local action plans drawn up by local people working jointly with agencies and the local authority with a key facilitation role played by the local strategic partnership (LSP), Bradford Vision. The action plans feed into an annual cycle of area-based conferences that lead to the production of area action plans for each constituency in the district. Each newly emerging local planning group receives an initial sum of £5,000 to help it get established and involve a spectrum of local people and agencies, followed up by a further £20,000 for the first phase of implementation.

The same support is available to communities of interest, who are encouraged to identify their particular issues and proposals for action. Action plans from communities of interest are brought together to form a composite communities of interest plan, which in combination with the area action plans, are fed into strategic partnerships and other decision-making bodies. Communities of interest across the district are in varied levels of organisation; some do not have any co-ordinating body that can pull together information about their community. Innovative outreach work is being carried out, for example with African, Philipino, Italian, Kurdish and gypsy traveller groups to help involve them in the planning process.

By early 2005, 11 communities of interest action plans had been completed with another 15 in the pipeline. The support for communities of interest is co-ordinated by the Communities of Interest Working Group, which involves both statutory agencies and representatives. The Working Group has set up a website and Communities of Interest Learning Forum.

Social enterprise

Social enterprises can be defined as:

businesses with primarily social objectives whose surpluses are principally reinvested for that purpose in the business or in the community, rather than being driven by the need to maximise profit for shareholders and owners.

Social enterprises share many of the features and problems of community and voluntary groups and can be seen as part of the voluntary and community sectors (Home Office, 2004b). For many people, being active in their local community group and taking on a key role such as treasurer or chair is a good stepping stone to starting a social enterprise.

The term 'black and minority ethnic' refers to a range of communities of interest of strongly contrasting economic situations, faiths and cultural norms and this will involve different support in different communities.

Many black and minority ethnic (BME) groups are of a self-help nature where they have developed in response to particular community needs. BME groups have, in many cases, been a lifeline to their own communities in providing services with close links to their members.

Capacity building with communities of interest generally needs flexibility to recognise where people are at in terms of confidence and collective organisation. Bringing people together to share experiences in a safe space is important. It's a slow process and needs time to build trust and relationships; it is skilful work involving community development skills.

Faith groups

Faith groups can also be seen as a particular type of a community of interest. Faith groups, centres and buildings have a key role to play as support organisations and can act as local focal points for the provision of community capacity building. In terms of inclusion, faith groups often bring in and involve members of communities who may not engage very much with mainstream activities or services. Their buildings and facilities are often based in areas of stress and can provide a familiar meeting place. Educational and pastoral work can be broadened to include community capacity building. Faith groups can also link community capacity building with cohesion activities to bring together people of different faiths through joint learning and enterprise. For example, usually local authority resources cannot be used directly to support religious activity per se, but associated group and social activities can act as a useful base for community capacity building.

Equally there are difficulties and barriers to consider:

- In some traditions, there is a strongly authoritarian basis to the spiritual leadership, which may conflict with the values of participation and accountability values of community development.

- Some groups can be inward looking and not very open to forming wider links.

- Some groups can be male dominated and exclude the equal participation of women.

These issues are discussed further in Chapter Four. There is great potential in work with and through faith groups to contribute to and participate in community capacity building. Given this potential and the increased focus on faiths as a part of community cohesion strategies, there is an argument to identify, as well as the community and voluntary sectors, an additional *faith sector*. Identifying it in this way does have the advantages of helping faith groups to see themselves as part of a wider movement and recognising the support and opportunities that faith-based groups provide in our communities. The recognition of a faith sector is still in debate and time will tell if the phrase gains wider usage.

Networks

The voluntary and community sectors also include *networks*, made up of groups, organisations or individuals. They may take the form of federations and coalitions or be much more loosely structured. At local street level, informal social networks are important forms of support and exchange. In many cases such local networks remain invisible, unnamed and unknown to authorities yet provide a crucial bedrock of social support.

Networks, both formal and informal, are especially important in community action.

- They can attract and involve marginalised people – many communities of interest are organised through networks.

- They can be a channel for learning and exchange – encouraging informal sharing of experience, contacts and skills.

- They are ways for minority groups to relate to each other without losing their own identity.

- They can be a power-base for community and voluntary groups – where groups come together to organise their own capacity building.

Consequently planning capacity building needs to consider the role and needs of networks. A useful definition is:

> *'Networks – including associations, movements and coalitions – are semi-formal groupings in which each member organisation remains autonomous in its activities, but where enough common ground exists to establish shared agendas. Networks are rarely rigid or hierarchical and are an implicit challenge to territorial or possessive attitudes towards handling of information and power. Dynamic networks may see diversity as their source of strength. At the same time they powerfully demonstrate that collaboration and cooperation are essential to development.'*

(Eade and Williams, 1995, p. 359)

Networks can bring together groups and organisations of different sizes and backgrounds and are based in and span both the voluntary and community sectors. A key development in many districts over the last few years has been the growth of community empowerment networks funded by the Government's Single Community Programme. These have been established to bring together voluntary and community groups in order to represent them in the local strategic partnership as well as other key partnerships.

Capacity building needs to consider the needs of networks, not just groups

Networking with IT

Computer-based networks are becoming popular, where people are in touch through emails and websites. Increasingly groups use computer-based e-mail contacts to create and run networks. For example, a residents' action group in Peckham, London has successfully used this method as its main form of communication and organising. However, in such forms of organising there is the need to look at who has access to computers, and who is communicating with whom – whether in practice the communication is limited to a band of people who are computer literate (Eade, 1997).

Networking

A *network* is a form of organisation – this is in contrast to *networking* which is a process, though the two are often confused. Networking is especially important in community capacity building because a fundamental feature is that it involves community groups themselves sharing knowledge and experience rather than relying on outside trainers, advisers or consultants. The question is – how does this process happen in practice and what needs to be done to enable its development?

First it's helpful to define the range of functions networking can include (Gilchrist, 2006):

- exchanging information and views

- joint working on a campaign to mobilise support and influence policy

- co-ordination of work in one area or district so as to avoid unnecessary duplication

- exchanging skills and learning

- giving support and building confidence

- developing a sense of common purpose

- representing an area or interest group in a consultation or partnership.

> The best part of the training course was the informal conversations with other experienced residents

If using networks and networking as a channel for capacity building, it is important to consider carefully who is being contacted and involved. Some local communities, often only a short journey apart, have dramatically different experiences, lifestyles and identities. In some cases, the bonds and bridges that bind people together do not extend across boundaries of gender, age, ethnicity, religion, class and education. Consequently if using networks as a channel for capacity building, there is a need to consider issues of access and diversity.

Active citizenship

The voluntary and community sectors are also a base for people being involved as active citizens. *Active citizenship* was introduced in the previous Chapter. It is about a wide range of activities and forms of involvement including, for example, people in their street, neighbourhood or community of interest:

- helping a neighbour

- getting involved in a community group

- joining a partnership as a community representative

- being on a voluntary sector management body

- taking on a public role, such as a parish councillor or magistrate.

It consequently spans the full range of voluntary and community sector activity as discussed so far, as well as including other forms of civic and public representation not necessarily a part of the VCS. For example, being an active citizen could include being an elected member or magistrate, neither of which would usually be seen as being based in the VCS. In addition, many people who work in the public or private sector may get involved in volunteering through work-based schemes – such activity could be seen as active citizenship. Consequently it needs to be concluded that active citizenship is:

- strongly rooted in the voluntary and community sectors but also spans other sectors

- a useful concept that can inform how the planning of capacity building is approached.

The extent of active citizenship in Britain

The extent of active citizenship has been identified in an interesting report written by Paul Whiteley, drawing on the Census of 2001 and the Citizens Audit of Britain 2000, which was a very extensive analysis of participation carried out across Britain (Whiteley, 2004). Out of an adult population of 44 million in Great Britain, the Census revealed that 2 million people belong to a residents', housing or neighbourhood organisation. The term 'belong to' includes a range of levels of participation, from merely paying a subscription to being an active member. About one in five people belong to an 'informal network of friends or acquaintances' who meet on a regular basis, for example a pub quiz team, book reading group, parent/toddler group, or child care group.

- A significant finding is that just under half of the people who are involved in such informal community activities are not members of any organisations – in other words often different people participate formally from those who participate informally.

- A key observation is that there is not much evidence that ethnicity is linked to informal participation, since ethnic minorities are 'as involved as the ethnic majority'.

- A further finding is that, based on analysis of local authority areas, levels of participation of communities across the country vary significantly in terms of time spent in voluntary activity per month.

- In particular, areas that have lower rates of participation have a moderately strong correlation with higher rates of robbery and car crime.

Active citizenship: questioning the concept

It is also important to take a critical look at active citizenship. There are questions as to who mainly benefits from increased levels of active citizenship. Some difficulties with the concept are:

- Whose agenda is it based on?

- Is more active citizenship always a good thing?

- Does it individualise the idea of acting in communities rather than focusing on working collectively?

- Will it have any real meaning for people who align themselves more with their own group, culture or religion?

- Who decides where support is needed to strengthen certain forms of active citizenship – and why?

- Is active citizenship changing the relationship between the individual and the state?

- What is the relationship between increased active citizenship and civil renewal? Do we need enhanced political processes and institutions as much as enhanced citizenship?

- How representative are active citizens who come forward to influence decisions on behalf of others in their community?

In particular there is a need to link active citizenship to accountable and more collective forms of community representation – the Active Citizenship Framework described in Resource Three is one way of attempting this.

Debate and research is needed to address these key questions. This book promotes the position that active citizenship is certainly an initiative that is on the policy agenda and therefore needs to be considered and responded to.

Diagram 2: *Some of the key features of the voluntary and community sectors*

The picture so far

In combination with the key themes and features of the voluntary and community sectors discussed so far, we can create a visual picture of how it all holds together. Diagram 2 shows some of the central features.

● There are two sectors – the voluntary sector and the community sector but no clear dividing line between them.

● Communities of interest and networks are based in both sectors.

● Active citizens are a part of and come from both sectors as well as originating in the wider community.

Sources of capacity building

So far we have given a very broad outline of the nature of the voluntary and community sectors. In addition, for voluntary organisations and community groups, there are key sources of community capacity building that need adding to the picture:

● infrastructure organisations based in the voluntary and community sectors

● voluntary organisations and community groups and networks

● community anchor organisations

● partnerships

● local authorities

● public sector organisations

● private sector organisations

● further and higher education institutions.

Firm Foundations

In December 2004, the Home Office launched its new policy initiative called Firm Foundations, the Government's framework for community capacity building (Home Office, 2004b). It forms part of the civil renewal agenda and focuses on the needs of community groups and active citizens. The Government completed its review of its support for community capacity building at the end of 2003 and consulted on its findings. Firm Foundations builds on the findings of the review and sets out a cross-departmental plan to support community capacity building more effectively. Firm Foundations follows Change Up, the national strategy to support the development of the voluntary and community sectors.

The Firm Foundations report includes a definition of community capacity building – the same as that used in this book – which was consulted on widely across the country. The report suggests that investment in community capacity building will have a positive impact on governance, sustainability, social capital and cohesion. The report identifies four priorities for action by Government as the basis of change:

- the development of a much broader range of learning opportunities for community engagement including citizens, communities, professionals and policy makers

- efforts to build community anchor organisations. These can take many forms but will address the needs of their area in a multi-purpose way

- the promotion of local action planning as a tool for involving citizens and community groups in the shaping of services

- enhanced collaboration at local, regional and national level, working through existing networks and partnerships, to make more effective use of the resources already available.

A linked initiative is the Active Learning for Active Citizenship programme which has established learning hubs around the country (Woodward, 2004).

Planning capacity building in any district or community will need to be based on an assessment of the current level of support provided. As discussed below, as well as from within the voluntary and community sectors, various forms of support for community capacity building can be provided by public sector organisations and partnerships.

- The term *infrastructure* clearly refers to those VCS organisations whose *main role* is carrying out some or all of the core functions described below, page 34. This will make *infrastructure* easier to identify and define.

- A much wider range of voluntary and community organisations, public sector agencies, partnerships and some private sector organisations may also contribute to providing various forms of what we can call *support*, much of which will help to build the capacity of the VCS. When they carry out this role, it is helpful to identify them as support organisations.

- Overall, the level of support in any district or community will be made up of a combination of infrastructure and support organisations.

- A key aspect of this is support given directly between groups themselves, which is a central element of community capacity building.

- Some of this support for community capacity building may be well planned and resourced and on a substantial scale, as provided by some local authorities.

- In some primary care trusts it may consist of an outreach team that works to build the capacity of community groups involved in health issues.

- In other cases, it may be of a very limited nature and marginal to how the organisation works, but still of significant value to the VCS.

- It may be a funding scheme to support capacity building, run by a regeneration partnership or a private company that operates a mentoring scheme, linking up managers with key members of community groups.

The *nature* of such support is explored further in Resource Five. The main *sources* of support for community capacity building are now looked at in turn. Two general points first:

- The quality and effectiveness of support will vary, depending partly on its source. Some organisations may provide support but are relatively out of touch with the needs of community and voluntary organisations.

- Those sources based directly in the voluntary and community sectors will be more directly aware of needs and issues. This will need to be born in mind in planning and using different sources of support.

Identifying the overall level of support in any one neighbourhood or district is discussed in Chapter Six.

The voluntary and community sectors infrastructure

A key source of capacity building is the voluntary and community sectors' own infrastructure. So what is meant by the term *infrastructure*?

Generally this term refers to an identifiable number of both voluntary and community organisations whose main function is to provide a variety of service roles for front-line VCS organisations. In many areas this role is carried out by councils for voluntary service (CVSs) – nationally there are over 350 CVSs.

Voluntary and community infrastructure organisations are those based in the VCS that play advisory, representative, policy making and capacity building role for other voluntary and community organisations. The term *infrastructure* refers only to those organisations that are part of the voluntary and community sectors.

Some infrastructure organisations are generic, aiming to provide support to the full range of the VCS operating in a particular geographic area. Generic infrastructure organisations usually consist of councils for voluntary service and rural community councils as well as, in some cases, larger community associations, development trusts, particular projects and charities. As an illustration, in Leeds, with a population of approximately two-thirds of a million, over 300 staff are employed by VCS infrastructure organisations.

Other infrastructure organisations may be specialist in that they relate to a particular part of the VCS, such as black and minority ethnic groups or a particular area of the district. The specialist role could consequently be one of several, based on:

- geographical area – particular neighbourhood or rural area

- type of issue – health, housing etc

- type of group – BME, tenants' groups, community of interest etc

- type of activity – such as volunteering or management.

In any one district, infrastructure organisations will have mainly built up organically over time. In some cases there may be duplication and their roles may overlap. The National Council for Voluntary Organisations (NCVO) encourages infrastructure bodies to work together to ensure that innovation and good practice is disseminated and resources shared on the basis of particular organisational needs (NCVO, 2003). NCVO proposes the following list of core functions in relation to local infrastructure. The term *local* here refers to the local authority area:

- **voice** – providing representation for their membership to funders, government and others

- **support** – for capacity building

- **best practice and advice** – promoting best practice and providing specialist advice

- **interface** – providing access for members to other agencies

- **co-ordinating and networking** – both horizontally and vertically between members and with other organisations

- **brokering** – identifying opportunities for organisations to work together.

This useful list helps to analyse the range of roles potentially carried out by the VCS infrastructure in any one district. Significantly for our area of concern, *capacity building* is only one of a number of key functions. Some of these functions may be provided by regional or national voluntary and community sector organisations, including regional forums and networks.

Change Up

The Change Up framework provides a ten-year vision of how local infrastructure would be organised – *local* in this context means district or borough. The vision is of infrastructure delivering both generalist and specialist infrastructure functions in every district by 2008. Both Change Up and Firm Foundations can play key roles in the development of neighbourhood and district-wide strategies and the planning of capacity building in the voluntary and community sectors. The Change Up report published in mid-2004 specifically recognises that Firm Foundations will be a parallel report and 'sit alongside it'. Change Up is certainly not just about developing the community and voluntary sectors' ability to deliver services, though it can be seen as having that as its main focus (Home Office, 2004c).

Rural infrastructure

Infrastructure organisations in rural areas may face a particular set of difficulties in providing their services:

- the dispersed nature of rural communities

- poor transport links

- low levels of networking between groups and between areas

- low take up of training and IT

- small communities that lack a 'critical mass' of volunteers

- a lack of understanding of diversity issues in some areas

- generally higher costs in delivering equivalent services.

From *Change Up* (Home Office, 2004c)

Voluntary organisations and community groups

In any one neighbourhood or district, there will also be community groups and voluntary organisations that provide some support to other such groups but not to the extent where they can be defined as part of the infrastructure. This is where there are community groups and voluntary organisations who provide some capacity building support but whose main role is providing a range of other activities and services. The support may be formal in nature – such as a busy community centre running some training for local groups as an addition to its normal range of activities. It can also be more informal support directly between groups. This can be a crucial form of exchange and is often unrecognised in planning capacity building. It may happen through networks, through joint working between groups or, for example, through a local mentoring scheme that links people from more experienced groups with those just starting out. In some cases this will involve community and voluntary organisations that are based in more than one district.

Community anchor organisations

At local neighbourhood and parish level, Firm Foundations proposes that capacity building can be organised in addition through what are called community anchor organisations. These can take many forms but will have four common features. They:

- are controlled by local residents and/or representatives of groups

- address the needs of their area in a multi-purpose way

- are committed to the involvement of all sections of the community

- facilitate the development of communities in their area.

The actual form they take in any one area will vary depending on local needs and what is there to build on – it may be a community centre, development trust, community association, local federation of groups or village hall. In practice, community anchor organisations may be a source of small grants, employ community workers, act as a venue for learning activities and be a physical hub and meeting place. Some neighbourhoods may just have one such hub; others may have more than one. Firm Foundations promotes the idea of such hubs developing an asset base to generate income.

Partnerships

Partnerships are a key way for public sector organisations as well as VCS organisations to contribute to community capacity building. In addition, through government funding schemes, government offices and departments can have a major role to play in guiding the use of central government resources at local level. This support is often channelled through partnerships in different settings. There are three main types in this context.

Area-based

Many local partnerships, for example, those using New Deal for Communities funding, have extensive experience of supporting and directly organising community capacity building. This can be both through specific projects and activities or where capacity building is integrated into other specific regeneration programmes. For example, a housing project may integrate capacity building for local tenants' associations into the development budget.

Strategic

As the overarching strategic body at district or county level, local strategic partnerships (LSPs) obviously have key co-ordinating roles to play in capacity building. Some LSPs directly employ staff to organise capacity building programmes, often linked to neighbourhood renewal and cohesion initiatives.

Issue- or service-based

In addition, within LSPs there are issue- or service-based partnerships, based on strategic themes such as housing, environment or child care. They vary in structure and resources: some have large budgets for service delivery programmes. Through their own policy initiatives or driven by central government funding criteria, many such partnerships fund and support capacity building, usually linked directly to their own targets and objectives.

The role of local area agreements is discussed in Chapter Two.

Local authorities

Local authorities have a key role to play in providing support for capacity building in communities. This can be through, for example, dedicated funding schemes to enhance the strength of the voluntary and community sectors or through employing an advice team. Such functions are usually linked to a community engagement strategy or policy on commissioning services. The ODPM's ten-year vision for local authorities supports such initiatives. In particular, the policy document *Why Neighbourhoods Matter* places capacity building in the context of enhanced area-based service management (ODPM, 2005a).

The private sector

Both large and small private sector organisations have much to offer in supporting community capacity building. This can include, for example, funding directly or through a linked trust, the provision of free or subsidised professional expertise, staff time in volunteering roles and access to equipment and meeting space. Often companies are interested in developing a relationship with a particular group or project rather than being a distant provider of resources. The relationship can be beneficial to both parties but obviously needs to be established on a clear basis where expectations and roles are made explicit.

EXAMPLE

Help from the private sector

The Blacon Project is a community regeneration initiative based in Chester where a locally-based credit card company has been a useful source of capacity building support. The company has provided for local groups:

● financial advice on accounts and business planning

● access to its solicitors for advice on leases and incorporation

● access to its building contractors and technical advisors

● regular income from the Give as you Earn scheme.

The support, among other things, fitted in with the company's staff development objectives, so both parties benefited.

Further and higher education

Institutions involved in teaching and research have great potential to act as a source of support for community capacity building. Some colleges and universities, within their lifelong learning provision, provide more specialist community education which is based on the learning needs of community workers and groups. Short course provision on management and communication skills, for example, can be a useful source of skill development. Some organise community-based projects to work jointly with community organisations, and student placements can, with appropriate choice and supervision, be a useful source of skill and knowledge sharing. Assisting groups with research work and developing research skills are useful ways of using the specific resources of higher education in community settings.

EXAMPLE

The University of Bradford's approach to community engagement

The University of Bradford has set up a systematic approach to engaging with communities across the District of Bradford and surrounding areas. Using finance from the Higher Education Innovation Fund, in 2004 it commissioned research to identify the potential for closer working with communities. A new Centre for Community Engagement has been established to act in a co-ordinating role and bring together a wide range of community-based initiatives the University is involved in. Community associates are based in a number of University schools to develop projects around community engagement. The team's work includes conferences and workshops, organised jointly with voluntary and community sector networks. The underlying policy agenda is broader than widening participation and based on a corporate commitment to be a *university at the heart of its communities*. The use of research to inform planning, the coordination of activities across the whole institution as well as a commitment to evaluation of impact are some of the particular features of Bradford's approach. More information is available on www.bradford.ac.uk.

Organising support for community capacity building

The Firm Foundations framework provides some useful principles to underpin actions to expand and improve support for building community capacity:

- **Adopt a community development approach** – this involves collective action, working with communities to identify needs and taking action to meet them. As a way of working it helps to draw marginalised and excluded groups into the process of change.

- **Recognise and build on what exists** – recognising the assets and strengths of groups, networks and leaders and using these strengths as the starting point for development. This principle needs to inform all stages of support and planning of community capacity building.

- **Take the long view** – invest in support for communities in ways that lead to long-term sustainable structures and relationships. This means recognising that effective building of strengths is often a long-term process and not a quick fix.

- **Ensure support is available at local levels** – if communities and citizens are to get the support they need it must be within easy reach, within their community of interest, neighbourhood or parish. The key components of such local support are looked at in Chapter Six.

- **Take a broad view of learning** – this will need to address the learning needs of people as volunteers, activists, group members, active citizens, representatives, councillors and leaders. Learning may well take place in a wide variety of ways and settings.

- **Embrace diversity** – one size will not necessarily fit all – different solutions will be needed depending on the context. Involving marginalised groups may mean working with communities of interest rather than focusing only on geographical communities.

(Adapted from *Firm Foundations*, Home Office, 2004b, page 8)

Completing the picture

So we can now add to the overall picture by adding support based in the various *sources* of community capacity building. The main additional points represented in Diagram 3 are:

- the *infrastructure* is clearly based in the voluntary and community sectors

- partnerships, public and private sector organisations, as well as higher and further education institutions, can and do provide a range of capacity building *support*

- community and voluntary organisations, including community anchor organisations, can be a key part of the range of support.

Please note at this point we are explaining support for the voluntary and community sectors (VCS). The VCS itself provides a wealth of skills, knowledge, experience and expertise for the public and private sectors: this theme is developed in Chapter Five.

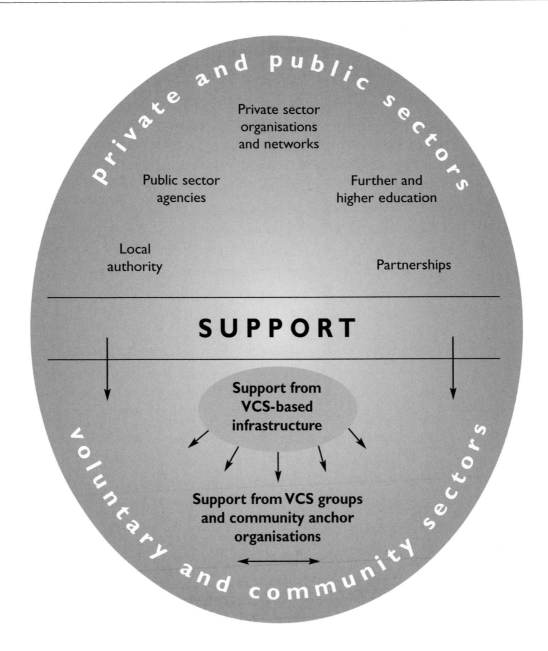

Diagram 3: *Sources of capacity building for the voluntary and community sectors*

Concluding points

This chapter has introduced some of the complexities of the voluntary and community sectors. Key concluding points are:

● Understanding the scale and diversity of the VCS is especially important, as is appreciating the innovative work being carried out with and by communities of interest.

● Equally, active citizenship and networks are key elements of the VCS and the wider picture.

● While the VCS' own infrastructure is central to support for capacity building, other organisations can also play key roles.

Chapters Two and Three have described the environment within which community capacity building occurs and can inform its objectives and practice. The practice of community capacity building is now looked at in the next Chapter.

The Story

One month on, and Dave had already volunteered to become the External Relations Secretary in the MS Action Group. Oh well, he'd said to himself, at least a grand sounding title, and he got to make use of some of his background in publicity and media work. The assertiveness course had been a big stepping stone for him – in three sessions so far, they were getting on well as a group, sharing a lot and, well, a lot of pain and anguish about MS and people's reaction to it. The group had really gelled and the trainer – a person who had her own problems in life – had shared a lot with the group too, and been a real human being. Jimmy was having a bad patch with his eyesight, but doggedly committed to the cause – helping the group to set up the centre, with the idea it would support all MS people across the borough, whether signed up members or not. 'Great idea, who knows how we'll pay for it!' he'd joked ...

So becoming External Relations Secretary was a real boost – it meant Dave got to meet important people. The first biggy was meeting someone high up from Social Services – Gita Patel, a hard-nosed, no-nonsense manager they said, who apparently was new to the job, and on her first ever visit to the group. So it was to be a meeting with her and the MS Action Group 'Executive' – the inner core of the group with himself included. He had been asked to 'chair' the meeting and the idea was to talk about the role of the group. 'Yes', he thought, 'that sounded demanding! Who knows how I will be healthwise that day?'

The practice
– building community capacity

Many people in communities are involved in local activity, self help, volunteering and community action, providing services and contributing to local decision-making. Groups, networks and organisations bring a wealth of skills, knowledge and experience to partnerships, programmes and projects. Many activists, volunteers and leaders are asking for help to further build their skills and many groups are increasingly interested in developing their organisations and networks. Chapter Four looks at these issues by focusing on more practical aspects of community capacity building.

Introduction

Across the country there is a wide range of initiatives, such as training, mentoring, action learning and organisational development work with groups and networks. How can we understand and support the effective planning of such a diverse range of activities, projects and programmes? Chapter Four describes community capacity building by dividing it into four simple headings:

● Building skills

● Building organisations

● Building involvement

● Building equality.

These four themes are based on experience of working with communities and draw on a widely used approach called ABCD (Barr and Hashagen, 2000). They are a useful way of understanding and planning community capacity building; there are also other approaches that are equally useful.

In Chapter Six, these issues are taken further by looking at how capacity building can be systematically planned, both with groups and at neighbourhood or district levels. Here we look at development needs and focus mainly on groups based in the community sector, rather than larger voluntary organisations, though there is obviously some overlap. Chapter Four starts by looking in a practical way at the skills and knowledge many groups want to develop. So firstly it's about skills …

Building skills

Building skills is about the skills, knowledge, experience, ways of working, confidence and empowerment of people; the term 'skills' is used here as a shorthand term for this range of attributes.

The aim of *building skills* is for people as active citizens and in community groups and networks to take active and leading roles in their communities and be effective as volunteers, good neighbours, members of community organisations, groups and networks and as representatives, community leaders or social entrepreneurs.

In this context, we mean skills for community involvement and action, not the skills needed by individuals to get a better job – though community capacity building may often have that as an additional outcome. Here our main concern is with people who are involved in community groups, rather than the development needs of paid staff in voluntary organisations. Examples of skills, knowledge, experience and abilities needed for effective group-based community activity are given in the box below. This is based on the experience of many community groups, networks and leaders (Skinner, 1997).

Checklist on skills, knowledge and abilities needed in the community sector

- [ ] management of people, money, assets and resources
- [ ] presentation and communication skills
- [ ] being able to listen and learn
- [ ] planning and vision building
- [ ] fundraising and accessing resources
- [ ] knowledge and practice in equality and diversity
- [ ] skills in negotiation
- [ ] being an accountable and effective community representative
- [ ] conflict resolution, teamwork and committee skills
- [ ] entrepreneurial behaviours, risk taking and problem solving
- [ ] evaluation skills
- [ ] skills in managing volunteers and giving practical support
- [ ] skills in accessing specialist information
- [ ] knowledge of how local authorities, agencies and partnerships work and plan their activities
- [ ] understanding local democracy
- [ ] confidence and self-worth
- [ ] a critical ability
- [ ] an understanding of power and influence.

It's quite a list! It demonstrates what demands are often put on unpaid hard-working members of groups, especially where they become representatives on public bodies and strategic partnerships.

The skills checklist can form the basis of identifying new learning needs. This will involve recognising existing skills, knowledge and abilities and identifying what else is required.

The learning needs a community group has may vary depending on:

- the general **stage** of development the group is at – whether it has just got going or is well established

- the **type** of group – the needs, for example, of a self-help support group will be very different from a community centre management committee; networks may well have specific needs, different from those of individual groups

- the **background** of the group – a group formed by newly arrived refugees, for example, may have particular support needs

- the **cultural identity** of the group – some black and minority ethnic groups may request particular areas of capacity building

- the current **objectives** of the group – a group with ambitious objectives to start a new project may generate new learning needs

- the **demands** placed on the group – for example, by funders for increased monitoring and by partnerships for accountable representation

- the **opportunities** available to the group – for example, to get involved in new activities such as neighbourhood planning or new links with other groups.

The experience of many community workers suggests that there is no clearly defined set of stages that groups go through, with different needs associated with each stage. A newly established group may need training to clarify roles such as chair and treasurer but equally a group established for several years may need to improve its clarity about such roles. The reality of effective learning and change in and with groups shows there is no set mechanistic solution as to what particular skills development is needed when.

> Capacity building is about releasing and
> using the skills, knowledge, talent and organisation
> that already exists in communities

Certainly, newly established groups or groups embarking on setting up new projects involving significantly increased demands and changed activities may need to build specific individual and organisational strengths to match the new challenges. At this macro level groups will recognise they may need support to make a key transition. Examples of such support during transitional periods are given in the box below.

The learning needs of a group will also depend on the existing skills, knowledge and experience, much of which may be untapped or underused. Consequently, a key aspect of the 'learning' process may be identifying and facilitating the use of the resources the group already has.

EXAMPLES

Examples of support tailor made for transitions

- The Housing Association Charitable Trust runs a funding programme in two stages to develop the skills and organisational abilities of partnerships involved in refugee housing. Phase one makes £5,000 available to ten selected partnerships for them to identify their aims, develop systems and complete action plans. Phase two awards £50,000 over two years for implementation of the plans with on-going capacity building. Integral to the whole programme is a philosophy that values the assets that refugees bring to the process.

- The London School of Economics has produced a resource pack to help community groups identify the stages they need to go through in setting up a new project. This identifies seven main stages and has useful checklists to consider. The pack is written in down-to-earth language and provides sources of information on further help and support. Copies can be downloaded from the LSE website www.lse.ac.uk/LSEhousing

Helping groups identify their learning needs

Some key pointers to use in the practical work of involving groups in identifying their learning and development needs are:

- Build relationships and trust – it's about getting to know the group and building good will.

- Start from needs and strengths – it involves really listening to what people are saying they need as well as valuing and facilitating the use of existing skills and experience.

- Avoid hit and run – learning and change does not happen over night – it needs medium and long-term support, not the short-term fix.

- Look at access – in terms of blocks to participation created by physical and cultural barriers.

- Base your work on principles – these are discussed later in this Chapter.

This initial list sounds reasonable enough – but what are the implications for managers of staff and resources involved in such work?

- It will take time – especially to involve less confident, excluded and so called hard to reach groups.

- It requires particular skills – in working with groups, in establishing relationships, in understanding learning processes and in bringing out and using existing skills the group already has.

- It needs planning – to look at how such work on identifying learning needs is prioritised.

An overview of practical methods of assessing learning of needs in groups is given in Resource Four.

The Learning Curve

The Learning Curve originated in the national neighbourhood renewal strategy and was published by the Neighbourhood Renewal Unit in the ODPM in 2002 (ODPM, 2002). It sets out a programme for supporting residents, practitioners, civil servants, professionals and organisations to gain the skills and knowledge needed for effective neighbourhood renewal. It has had substantial resources dedicated to it through the Single Community Programme, though these funds are by definition limited on a national scale to neighbourhood renewal areas. It is a broad-based strategy on community learning, looking at both the needs of residents and professionals. It does not explicitly focus on the needs of community and voluntary organisations in any great depth, though many have directly benefited from the Single Community Programme.

Forms of learning

Building skills will usually involve organising learning in some practical form. The actual form the learning takes – whether for example, course-based training or a mentoring scheme – may vary depending on the needs of the group and available resources. Community capacity building in practice displays a range of adult learning methods; this range is important to reflect that adults have different learning styles and different cultural approaches to participating in learning.

The classic knee-jerk reaction is to put on course-based training, without really considering if it fits what is needed, responds to what the group is saying or builds on local experience. Considering the range of forms of learning available is consequently an important part of organising effective capacity building.

Forms of learning to build skills

- Course-based training
- Tailor-made training
- Workshops
- Action learning
- Visits
- Peer learning
- Information sheets
- NVQs
- Websites

- On-the-job coaching
- Placements and secondments
- Shadowing
- Online learning
- Guided reading
- Resource packs
- Mentoring
- Resident consultancies
- Community arts

The box above shows a range of forms used. Each form will have its particular advantages and disadvantages. Four forms are also looked at in the box overleaf in more detail to aid comparison.

● The distinction presented here between the different forms may not be so clear in practice but it useful to start in this way to help clarify the options.

● The choice of form should be made in consultation with the participants wherever possible.

Further information on forms of learning is provided in *Building Community Strengths,* a publication written by the author which is a more practical resource book (Skinner,1997). The aim here is to give an introduction and overview of what needs to be thought about and considered. Peer learning is similar to action learning, as shown from the two examples given, the main difference being that peer learning specifically involves people from a similar setting, whereas action learning may not.

Considering the range of forms of learning available is an important part of organising effective capacity building

Comparing forms of learning

Group-based training

● Designed and run specifically for an existing group
● Usually provided in response to requests from the group
● Tailor made to suit needs
● Usually based in group's own centre

Pros	Cons
● Because based on own site, likely to get more people from the group involved	● If the group is stuck with an inward-looking culture, mixing with members of other groups could be more effective
● Working with the whole group could also lead on to organisational development work	● As it is 'home-based', it may not be taken as seriously by participants
● For many community groups it is their first contact with training and because of understandable fears around 'education', may be the only initial route into adult learning	● Participants will not usually meet new people and make contacts
	● As a tailor-made course, it may not be accredited

Course-based training

● Often held in a more central venue involving members from several community groups
● Pre-set course
● Sometimes accredited

(continued)

Course-based training *(continued)*

Pros

- Wide range of experience and perspectives from the different groups
- Not specifically requested content so may introduce new ideas and skills
- Participants away from home area so may be more receptive to new ideas
- Participants may gain a qualification from accredited courses

Cons

- Pre-set course may have elements unrelated to some groups' needs
- Central location may put off some people who find travelling difficult
- May only attract participants who are already confident and more skilled
- If linked to assessment, may alienate people unfamiliar with process

Mentoring

- One-to-one support between two people from different organisations where one provides guidance, advice, guided learning, support and confidence building
- May involve private or public sector, community or voluntary sector providing the mentor

Pros

- Intensive learning
- Can provide more encouragement and support than course-based training
- Can provide role models of more successful organisations
- Personal and organisational links can lead to on-going networking

Cons

- In some cases can involve considerable staff time to set up and maintain

Visits

- Party from one group visits another group that can help it in its development
- Groups learn directly from each other
- Requires careful preparation, good organisation and systematic follow-up

Pros

- Can boost morale by inspiring a 'we can do that too' belief
- May lead to on-going links between groups

Cons

- Without adequate planning, visits can turn into sightseeing tours
- Host group may try to impress rather than share real experiences and problems
- The gap between the visiting group and the host group's stage of development, if too large, may backfire and be demoralising

EXAMPLE

Action learning in Durham

This example describes action learning and how the same learning method can be adapted to three different groups of participants.

Action Learning for Managers in Durham County was set up in 2004 as part of a national pilot organised by the National Association of Councils for Voluntary Service. Three action learning sets were run in turn for members of community groups, trustees from voluntary organisations and chief executives from local authorities. Group sessions were held monthly over six months. The learning was not content-based but achieved through critical reflection on current work practice and problems, carried out in a supportive group setting. Each learning set used similar methods:

● a facilitator to enable the group

● ground rules of confidentiality and listening

● presentations from each member on problems and progress in dealing with them

● critical examination of options and solutions

● an action points list that each member used as the basis of their progress between meetings.

All three learning sets resulted in increased confidence, energy, networking and on-going support between group members. The method is a way to use community development principles in a very practical and effective learning environment. The pilot showed positive results and the approach will be developed nationally through a facilitator training programme and handbook. For more information contact the National Association of Councils for Voluntary Service.

EXAMPLE

Peer learning in the West Midlands

This example describes an effective form of learning between staff of community empowerment networks within the West Midlands.

Regional Action West Midlands has helped to establish two learning groups for community empowerment networks. These peer support groups provide an opportunity to bring together staff of community empowerment networks to share experiences and collectively problem solve. They have one peer support group for community empowerment network co-ordinators and one for community chest managers and outreach workers. The meetings have a simple format. The agenda is constructed at the start of the meetings, so only live issues are discussed and the agenda belongs to those who are attending. At the end of the meeting, there is a quick area update to cover anything that hasn't been talked about. The middle section of the meeting is facilitated to ensure that individuals learn from each other, unpick local experiences and look for shared issues and then the group's collective experience is used to problem solve any particularly sticky issues. The group is able to absorb new members and it is kept fresh by having a learning item, where either a group member or the facilitator is asked to bring forward a theory or idea, that might be of use to others.

Building organisations

The development of skills, knowledge, confidence and abilities increases the capacity of people to act collectively through community groups, networks and organisations. However, community groups and networks are more than the individuals that make them up. They also consist of the organisational structures, systems and policies that help to create sustainability and accountability in community activity. Coalitions, federations and networks, where people and groups come together for joint action, also need effective organisation to achieve lasting impact. So the planning of community capacity building also needs to consider a second theme, of *building organisations* – building up the organisation itself.

Organisational development can support groups and networks where they want to develop their plans, structures, policies and systems to ensure they are being effective and achieving their aims. Organisational development is both an academic discipline and a practical approach to helping organisations grow; our concern is mainly with the latter (Mullins, 1993). Groups reach the point of asking for help with organisational development for a variety of reasons, such as:

● a crisis within the group has created the need for a review and changes in the organisation

● growth in the group's activities has led to the need for a new structure in how it operates

● members are unhappy with the group's ways of working and 'culture'

● a new opportunity or funding source has created new demands.

In other words, the reasons for getting help with developing the organisation can be positive or negative, and can be internally or externally driven. Equally, a request on identifying training needs in the group may lead to unearthing an underlying problem which needs addressing through wider organisational changes.

Examples of what community groups and networks may need are described in the box on the next page, which is based on what an organisation needs to be 'healthy' (adapted from Fowler, 1995). These are only examples under each heading and it is not an exhaustive list. Not all these will apply to any one group or network; the type of structure will vary depending on the type of group or network and its stated aims. Equally, it is wrong to assume groups naturally move from being small and less structured to being large complex community organisations. Many small community groups carry out valuable and efficient activities within their community with little formal structure.

The checklist shows the complexity of running a community organisation. It suggests that the skills of its staff, voluntary management committee or key members are only one part of a range of functions that are needed to keep the organisation going. This type of checklist could be used as the basis of questions to review how an organisation is doing. In practice, groups will vary greatly in their level of organisation; many groups will be operating very well without a clear 'vision' or many established systems – it depends a lot on the type of group and what it is trying to achieve. We are not proposing all these features need to be present in every case – it is an example of a checklist to use and adapt. Where funding and commissioning of services are involved, funders may request particular standards and want to ensure the organisation is 'fit for purpose' – this can place strains on a small organisation or group.

Many groups develop a new form of organisation without any outside help. In other cases, external assistance will be needed and can have many advantages.

A healthy organisation

Identity and values

- An underlying set of beliefs

Vision, mission and strategy

- A set of aims and objectives

Systems and structures

- An appropriate constitution and organisational basis such as being a trust or limited company

Policies and practices

- Policies on staff recruitment, management and financial control
- Clearly defined roles of leading positions in the organisation
- Policies on equal opportunities and diversity

Skills and abilities

- Key members, volunteers and staff equipped with the necessary knowledge, skills and ways of working

Communications and relationships

- Ways of communicating with members, users or residents
- The organisational culture that matches aims and values

Material and financial resources

- Equipment, buildings, funding, cash flow

The box opposite lists a range of options for groups to use in getting external help with organisational change. The pros and cons of using different sources of help are described in other publications (see for example Skinner, 1997). Whatever the background of the specialist, to work effectively with groups and networks, they will need some understanding of how community groups work and the processes involved. Community development work provides a core set of skills and competencies that can help to define what skills are needed to work effectively with community groups – see Resource Six.

Using the four themes

So far we have looked at community capacity building under the two headings of *Building skills* and *Building organisations*. This has created a way in to understand the needs of community representatives, groups and their members and to look at the organisational development of groups. But in practice community capacity building is not just a technical fix. It is not just about identifying gaps in skills and knowledge or areas of organisational development and addressing them. It is also about empowerment, about involvement and about basing practice on principles.

Getting help

Help with *building organisations* can come from a variety of sources:

- specialist advisers based in the voluntary and community sectors
- community development practitioners
- freelance funding advisors and consultants
- project and programme managers
- specialist staff in local authorities and agencies
- experienced group or network members
- residents as consultants and mentors
- business advisors
- researchers and trainers
- professionals based in the private sector.

We can introduce two further themes or 'building blocks' that address these issues. In combination, these four themes create a useful practical basis for understanding how community capacity building can be organised.

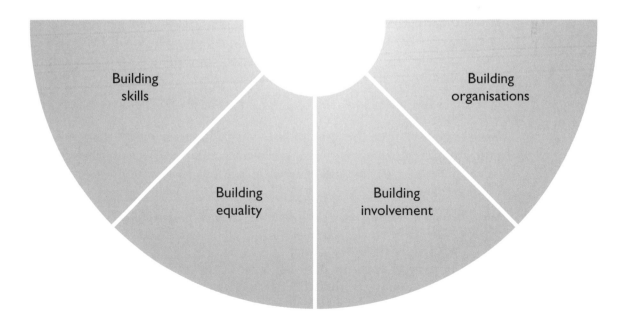

Diagram 4: *The four building blocks*

Building involvement

Building involvement is about activities, learning and change that focus on how individuals get involved in their communities. It's also about how community groups and networks involve people and contribute to local decision-making. *Building involvement* is consequently a wider process of learning and change than *building skills* or *building organisations*. It is the third key theme to consider in the practice and policy of community capacity building.

Involvement is a key issue in how communities are organised. In capacity building it can include looking at:

- **Access into the group:** how individuals get into groups, projects, centres and networks – this would include, for example, how open and welcoming the group is, how it makes contact with new people, how easy it is to gain access into the group or centre.

  I went down the centre and got ignored. Not going there again!

- **Participation in the group:** how groups interact with and include their users and members – this would include, for example, how the group is run, how it involves people, whether key roles are open over time for new members to take on.

  Betty's been our chair for years; she runs the group so we let her get on with it

- **Participation of the group in networks:** how networks contact, interact with and include individuals, community groups and communities of interest – this would include, for example, the ways networks are run and how they involve groups, whether they exclude certain groups, whether they act as a channel of information and exchange or as a barrier.

  That network meeting had the paid staff talking all the time and using fancy jargon – not for me!

- **Accountability of the group:** how the group relates to its membership, neighbourhood or community of interest – this would include, for example, to what extent it holds open public meetings and distributes information on its work, finds out about local needs and uses this information to inform its planning.

  We always run the annual bus trip – it's just apathy that no one comes any more

- **Representation of the group:** how community representatives or advocates represent their groups and networks – this would include, for example, how much they base their views on consultation and gathering of information and how they report back to their group or network.

  We never see Christina nowadays, now she's on that high level committee, mixing with the men in suits ...

These five issues will apply in different ways to different groups and networks. So *building involvement* is about working with individuals, groups and networks to help them look at and develop their policies, practices and procedures in terms of these types of issues. Community capacity building can help groups to tackle such issues and encourage ways of working that develop opportunities for change. Many people see *building involvement* as more important than *building skills* or *building organisations* as they view it as the key to empowerment and confidence.

The practical work with groups on *building involvement* can mean addressing a range of questions in a practical way. Here are some examples that go into more detail. Again flexibility is needed in using such questions, as they will not all necessarily apply to any one particular group.

- In what ways is the group accountable to its communities, members or users?

- Does it ever produce newsletters or hold open feedback meetings?

- Does it hold open annual elections to key positions?

- What approaches do groups use to find out about the needs of the local community or communities of interest?

- Does it organise consultation meetings?

- Is it involved in any outreach work?

- Does it collect or use information from surveys?

- How effectively does the group consult its members or neighbourhood about what they do?

- Does the group let local people know what it is doing?

- Are there opportunities to join? Who are these targeted at?

- Who in practice responds?

- Are there opportunities to take on key roles?

- How does the group support and train volunteers working with it?

- How does it support and train people acting in key roles such as chair, treasurer, secretary, publicity officer?

- How does it support and train people acting as representatives of the group on networks or partnerships?

Consequently the provision of community capacity building will need to address such issues, both in its content and how it is organised.

Groups may be leaving people out on the margins
or act as gateways to social support and collective action

The role of empowerment

Building involvement needs to be a people-centred process based on what is called *empowerment*. This is a much abused and misunderstood term but central to building involvement. We can paint a picture of empowerment as consisting of three key features:

- **Influence** – where groups and individuals have increasing control over decisions that affect them and the resources they need to achieve their aims.

- **Personal effectiveness** – a psychological experience involving development of a strong sense of self-worth and confidence.

- **Analysis** – a process of analysing and understanding the causes of discrimination and deprivation (Skinner, 1997).

The box below looks at this in more detail.

Empowerment

A useful way of identifying what empowerment means is to break it down into three key elements of confidence, critical ability and influence. Here we are looking at the empowerment of individuals involved in community activity.

Confidence

People who live in poverty, who suffer from discrimination, who face unemployment and have to cope with high levels of stress, often experience low levels of confidence and self-worth. For people to build their confidence, recognising the value of their experience is a key part of the change process. Many disability groups have got involved in confidence building in order to support their members in challenging patronising attitudes. Assertion training has tremendous potential to support people in community activity to be more direct, more in touch with what they want and how to get it. It is about developing skills and self-esteem in order to relate to others more effectively and negotiate from a position of strength.

Critical ability

Empowerment also means developing a critical ability in understanding in the causes of problems and deprivation in communities. This approach often takes inspiration from the work of Paulo Friere, a Brazilian activist. His approach can include exploring the dynamic of discrimination and how people internalise negative messages about their status and rights (Eade and Williams, 1995). This approach uses challenging questions, starting with people's own direct experiences and perceptions. Critical ability is an important part of community involvement – we cannot assume participation in neighbourhood renewal and other initiatives should lead to an easy or co-operative relationship where people do not sometimes question the process. Empowerment will involve critical dialogue and at times a challenge to prevailing attitudes and procedures, both in the public sector and in the voluntary and community sectors.

Influence

The third element of empowerment is about power. Real change in communities will need to address issues of power, whether in groups, networks, partnerships or agencies. It will need to be informed by an awareness of how power lies between different groups of people based on ethnicity, gender, disability, sexuality and class as well as other key factors. Does the chair of our group dominate the decision-making? Are network meetings organised without child-care that may exclude parents? Are decisions in partnerships made before the board meetings – or afterwards in the pub? These are the types of questions that raise the issues of power and influence.

In summary, it can be said that *empowerment is a process where people who are active in their communities experience greater influence over decisions that affect them, greater personal effectiveness and increased abilities in analysing their social and political environment.*

We have explored *empowerment* at some length because it is a term used widely yet rarely defined. It is often only vaguely addressed in capacity building where too often only the more tangible and technical aspects of building skills are catered for. There are many useful publications on the issue (see Eade and Williams, 1995). Effective capacity building needs to be informed by an understanding of *empowerment* in its planning and implementation. Empowerment is a key underlying principle in community capacity building, but it needs to be used in combination with other key values. We move on to look at these, by introducing the fourth building block.

EXAMPLE

Building capacity through the arts

In the Newlands Regeneration area of Bradford District, a community arts organisation called Artworks organised a programme of local activities that helped to build capacity and empower people. The overall aim of the Newlands Partnership, a Single Regeneration Budget-funded organisation, was to enhance the capacity of local people to contribute to regeneration. Artworks worked alongside a wide range of public sector agencies, voluntary organisations and community groups to offer a wide range of creative experiences including:

● taster sessions

● short-term projects passing on creative techniques

● consultancy activity using creative approaches to planning and organisational development.

An independent evaluation of the Newlands work demonstrated that the arts can be used to develop skills and expertise, providing a stimulus for people of different backgrounds to come together in dialogue. Artworks provided a creative alternative for agencies to engage residents in the regeneration process.

Building equality

The fourth theme to consider in community capacity building is called *building equality*. The term *equality* is used here to mean three key principles of:

● *equal opportunities*

● *diversity*

● *cohesion.*

These three key principles need to underlie and inform community capacity building and not just be an add on – *building equality* needs to be central to how capacity building is planned, funded and carried out, in whatever particular form of learning or support is adopted.

Building equality has a major role to play in understanding and organising capacity building. Basing support on the principles of equal opportunities, diversity and cohesion means that capacity building cannot just be a technical process of identifying a gap in skills or organisational abilities and addressing it. We now look at what this means in practice, taking each of the three principles in turn.

Let's face it – it's not a level playing field

Equal opportunities

Capacity building can support excluded groups in their activities to obtain a fair share in their neighbourhood or district, and strengthen groups of people who face discrimination to challenge what's going on. Unless these real life experiences are considered, capacity building may not address the underlying issues.

● Equality of access to services and resources is a key issue facing many communities. Some people experience discrimination and barriers to influencing and accessing services, which others take for granted.

● Within this context, the ability of excluded groups and communities of interest to influence and access resources and services is often affected by how organised the groups and their networks are.

● Action is needed to ensure that such communities are appropriately supported to build their level of skills and organisation.

Because of such issues, the balance of power also needs to be considered and understood in order to support effective change in communities. There are examples, particularly from Developing World development settings, where capacity building programmes have led to a strengthening of an already dominant group, such as a ruling group of men in a village where women are discriminated against (Eade, 1997). Alternatively in such cases, if handled well, there is a potential for capacity building to act as a catalyst for change and raise issues around gender and participation.

Capacity building cannot just be about *empowerment* – it needs to also be based on *equal opportunities* in its organisation and resourcing. Many groups are actively requesting help in developing both policy and practice in equal opportunities. This may be prompted by a desire for groups to be more open to the communities they are based in, or due to more functional reasons such as conditions attached to funding. Either way there are many progressive initiatives to build on.

Capacity building cannot just be about empowerment –
it needs also to be based on equality principles

Diversity

Diversity is the second principle within the heading of *building equality*. Considering issues of diversity in communities can inform how capacity building is organised and the style of delivery. It's about recognising the range of identities and interests that exist in neighbourhoods and networks and valuing people's different perspectives and needs. In particular, it's about appreciating that people learn in different ways and that they have a wealth of experience and ideas to share. Communities are complex and varied. Diversity, as a principle, means community groups and networks will need to work in ways that are sensitive to different interests and identities. As introduced in Chapter Three, the phrase *communities of interest* helps to understand how communities work. People in communities of interest may share an identity, for example, an ethnic identity such as being Polish or Ukrainian, or share an experience or concern, such as being a carer. These different life experiences will affect people's needs in terms of learning and support.

EXAMPLE

Women, leadership, participation and involvement

Over the last five years an organisation called Working for Change has developed capacity building for women in the West Midlands. The workshop-based approach was based on the recognition that many women still experience being marginalised and excluded from mainstream political activity. Working for Change took the view that while confidence building is a key component, it is not enough to create real and lasting change. 'We wanted to work with women to change this situation and ensure that they have the potential to access the places where decisions are made, priorities set and resources distributed.' The workshops included training and mentoring around citizenship, personal development, participation and political awareness. The workshops led to major shifts in women's lives, their perception of themselves and their abilities to influence decision-making.

- Some groups may need separate capacity building provision, for example, many south Asian women may prefer women-only sessions.

- Some people may feel more at home in places they already know; others may want to meet people from wider backgrounds and value a city centre location.

- Some groups may grow and develop their organisations in totally different ways from how the standard books on community development and project management describe the process – including this one!

- Equally there will be groups in communities and neighbourhoods who define themselves in ways that are divisive.

Being flexible, understanding people's backgrounds and building trust are all part of the approach, while challenging discrimination and exclusion in ways that really bring about change.

By applying the concept of diversity to all our lives, it helps to show *building equality* is not just about responding to the needs of 'disadvantaged minorities' but is a more positive movement involving celebration of the cultural and social diversity of neighbourhoods and communities.

Equal opportunities and diversity in community work

In this chapter we are exploring how building equality can inform the practice and policy of community capacity building. In addition, there is a complex area of debate as to how community work with groups addresses the two issues of diversity and equal opportunities. The dilemma is that many small groups in the community sector are formed specifically to support and involve people of a particular background or identify, such as an Asian women's group. Should such groups adopt a policy of being open to all? Some groups, such as disability groups, are by their very nature not open to all. How then can community workers tackle this issue? Some suggestions follow.

- The equal opportunities principle can still inform work with single identity groups but in a more limited way. For example, a women-only group may be encouraged to look at the age range of its members and whether women with disabilities have fair opportunities to participate.

- The equal opportunities principle can inform the overall approach to outreach work in the community sector. It could mean supporting communities of interest so they are better organised and more involved in decision-making. In other words, by building a broad spread of groups it can mean the sector as a whole provides equal opportunities for people to participate, rather than everyone being able to participate in every group.

- The equal opportunities principle can still be the basis of challenging more powerful, mainstream, dominant groups who may be excluding others, where there is no valid justification for the group to be single identity. This could be the basis of such an approach, as in the example quoted above on page 56 from the male dominated village.

A key to resolving these dilemmas is to be flexible in how equal opportunities is applied in group development and consider carefully in each group setting what is appropriate while in no way diluting the underlying values that inform the work.

Links

Diversity needs to be complemented by acceptance, understanding contact and joint working between communities. The Cantle report, published in December 2001, showed areas of the country in which different ethnic communities led *parallel lives* (Cantle, 2001). Cantle argued polarisation between communities needed cross-community initiatives to reduce tensions and increase understanding. The Denham report brought the Cantle report's findings together with those produced in Burnley, Oldham and Bradford and the recommendations formed the basis of government action (Denham, 2001). To address the cohesion agenda, community capacity building needs to be informed by initiatives that bring people together from different communities and backgrounds. Here the particular concern is with the need to build bridges, contacts and communication between groups of different backgrounds, beliefs and traditions. This needs to be much broader than just focusing on ethnicity; it needs also to be based, for example, on gender, sexuality, disability and age.

There seems to be no useful appropriate plain language term for building such contact between groups; the term *links* seems to be the best term available and is used here to mean initiatives that between different groups:

- increase understanding and tolerance

- reduce conflict and tensions

- encourage contact and communication

- support joint working and shared buildings.

In many such practical ways, groups and networks of different backgrounds and identities can interact and build effective relationships. This will be a part of building *stronger communities*, as discussed in Chapter Two. Such initiatives to develop links need to be developed in a context of explicit policies and practice that will achieve equality of access to services, resources and employment for different communities. In other words, discrimination needs to be tackled in an open and direct manner in parallel to initiatives that increase contact and links between different groups. Without addressing such disparities of power and advantage, such initiatives may fall prey to withdrawal and cynicism.

Developing links needs to consider not just people's backgrounds in terms of their culture and ethnicity but also their identity in terms of age, gender, sexuality, disability and so on. Some cohesion policies adopted by local strategic partnerships and local authorities do take this wider view rather than just limiting the perspective to ethnicity. In order to involve communities of interest, as discussed earlier, such a wider view will be crucial.

Community capacity building is a resource that can be used in a negative way to maintain the current patterns of power and privilege in communities. Alternatively it can be part of a movement that builds equality of opportunity, diversity and links between different communities and groups. The principles identified here are not an optional add on – they are essential to the effective organisation of support at the grass roots.

Building equality checklist

Here are the types of questions that can support addressing issues of equal opportunities, diversity and links in organising capacity building. It needs to be used with flexibility and sensitivity – not every question will apply to every group or situation.

- Is there recognition of different identities and perspectives within the way capacity building is organised?

- In capacity building activities, are groups of different backgrounds and identities linking with each other in ways to promote understanding and useful contacts?

- Is learning about different groups and cultures a part of capacity building content?

- What priorities are used to identify which groups are supported with outreach work?

- Are communities of interest involved in producing capacity building plans?

- Does capacity building strengthen already strongly dominant groups?

Concluding points

As shown, community capacity can be built by designing and organising support based on four simple headings – building skills, building organisations, building involvement and building equality. Chapter Six takes this further and looks at what this means in practical planning terms for how support and resources can be organised. There are three key concluding points for this chapter.

- The four building blocks themes can be seen as a useful framework for the effective support of community capacity building.

- They can be used to inform planning and provision at a variety of levels, from working just with one group, organising support in a neighbourhood or with a community of interest to strategic planning at local authority level. This is discussed in Chapter Six on planning.

- Using the four building blocks is a way to ensure that principles are embedded into capacity building planning and practice.

In summary, headings for these principles, as discussed, can be given as:

- Enhancing empowerment

- Supporting diversity

- Promoting equal opportunities

- Developing links.

In combination, these principles and the four building blocks can directly contribute to developing the features of a *strong community* described in Chapter Two. In practice, all aspects of increasing community strengths need to integrate these principles and address these issues. This is a wide process involving the public sector as much as community and voluntary organisations. We now move on, in the next chapter, to explore what this means in practice by exploring capacity building in relation to community engagement.

The four building blocks

The four building blocks used in this publication originate from three main sources:

- *Achieving Better Community Development*, known as ABCD, is an important evaluation and planning tool for community development now used widely across Britain. It was developed by the Scottish Centre for Community Development. It includes four key dimensions under the headings of Personal Empowerment, Positive Action, Community Organisation and Participation and Involvement. These are seen within ABCD as the core aspects of community development (Barr and Hashagen, 2000).

- *The Building Communities Partnership* in Bradford District used and developed the ABCD model in producing its community development strategy in 2000. It changed the four headings into more accessible terms of Building Skills, Building Organisations, Building Involvement and Building Equality (Building Communities Partnership, 2004).

- *Assessing Community Strengths* is a publication that describes a practical approach that can be used to identify a baseline of community capacity. It used the four themes from ABCD and the Building Communities Strategy and developed them into a framework for identifying the level of community capacity and support in neighbourhoods (Skinner and Wilson, 2002).

In combination these sources mean a wide range of practical experience and knowledge has gone into the ideas and principles contained in the four building blocks. By basing capacity building planning on the ABCD model, it means it can have community development principles firmly integrated into it, in both theory and practice.

The Story

It was 1.30 on a rainy Wednesday afternoon and Gita was nervous. The meeting was to start at 2 pm and she was already late. The MS group had turned out to be quite an experience that she hadn't planned for – they seemed very confident and a bit pushy. The set of papers they had sent in advance was surprisingly clear. One of their members, David Coney, was to be Chair ... she was beginning to realise that dealing with groups like these was going to be quite demanding. They seemed far more on the ball, informed and assertive than she had assumed. She felt out of her depth – was there training for this sort of thing? Yes, Human Resources – they would do that kind of thing – 'relating to communities' or something like that. As she parked her car for the meeting, she was wishing she'd already done it ...

Dave was nervous too – he hadn't been to meetings in this formal way for about two years, let alone chaired one. They had prepared, of course – in fact the trainer had used the forthcoming meeting to help them look at the doubts they had about it. 'We need to look at ourselves as individuals, at the group and how it's organised' she'd said. So they had all 'identified our training needs' – can't she use everyday language? That was last week and this was it, thought Dave – '2 pm, meeting the Head of Commissioning, a Social Services Senior Manager and who am I?' They had it all ready – the agenda, the cakes, the background information on their new proposal; Jimmy was amazing – he said he would give others a chance to take the lead, being an 'old dog' at all this. Dave had had a good long chat with him and got a lot from it. So OK Ms Patel, here we go – the MS Action Group is going to have an impact!

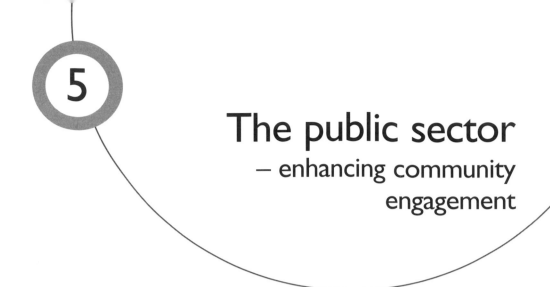

The public sector
– enhancing community engagement

Chapter Five is about the public sector – it's about how public sector organisations and partnerships involve and relate to communities. We take a hard look at community engagement and ask some basic questions. Why bother? What does community engagement lead to? Does it actually contribute to better services? Is capacity building part of community engagement? How does capacity building contribute to it? Chapter Five looks at what community engagement means in practice and provides a model that describes a range of options. It then moves on to describe how community engagement can be improved, building on the extensive good practice that already exists.

Introduction

The main arguments presented in this Chapter are:

- there are good reasons and clear evidence to show that partnerships and public sector organisations can benefit from community engagement

- there is a range of options available for community engagement for partnerships and public sector organisations that are much broader than consultation

- improving practice and policy in community engagement – what we call *agency capacity building* – can make use of the four building blocks themes

- supporting *community capacity building* is one of the options that are a part of effective community engagement.

This Chapter gives an introduction to these issues – and no, it is not yet another tool kit! It is not another 'how to' guide on community engagement, more an overview of what is needed, building on current good practice and policy. It describes, in basic outline, a range of approaches, with signposting to further information and websites. It mostly focuses on the public sector but also includes some examples of good practice from other sectors. Many partnerships and public bodies are involved in innovative initiatives to involve users and communities in the design and delivery of services – there is much good work to build on. We value this experience and use it to take a broad view of current issues in community engagement.

Community engagement seems to be the most useful term now being adopted widely in the public sector for describing a range of forms of contact and interaction with communities. These involve a number of terms, for example:

- consultation and participation
- supporting groups and using volunteers
- commissioning services
- involving community representatives
- joint working.

How can we make sense of such a wide range of options? The community engagement model described below, pages 65ff does this by providing categories that can be used for looking at practice and planning issues. We argue capacity building underlies and informs all the options in order to achieve effective community engagement.

Research on community engagement and governance

Research has identified common characteristics that underlie a wide spectrum of community engagement in the UK. They are:

- an emphasis on *accountability*, enabling communities and partners to hold institutions and policy makers to account

- a concern with the involvement of *multiple stakeholders* in new forms of partnership, enabling a wider ownership of decisions and projects

- a concern with *inclusion*, especially of minorities based on age and ethnicity seen as marginalised

- a concern with more *active and participatory forms of citizenship*, changing the roles from 'users to choosers' based on the notion of citizens who engage directly in the design and delivery of services.

The research was carried out by Gaventa, published in 2004, commissioned by the ODPM (Gaventa, 2004).

For many public sector organisations, some degree of community engagement, in at least how they design their services, is now a given. A key ODPM report using data from 216 local authorities showed approximately eight million people were involved in local authority initiated exercises using nineteen different methods for consultation, participation and decision-making (Birch, 2002).

For some agencies there is now no choice about involving communities and users in policy decisions, for example, where central government has tied funding streams to specific conditions concerning participation. Consequently many service managers are obliged to involve users and communities to some degree – whether they want to or not.

What are the advantages of community engagement?

Recent key policy statements from central government in combination provide eight good reasons why any one public sector organisation or partnership may wish to engage with communities – see box below. The good reasons are culled from three sources.

- An informative set of guidelines on engagement, produced by the Home Office in 2003 to inform other government departments, suggests five of the benefits listed. While devised for this specific governmental context, these are useful as potentially applying to many public sector organisations and partnerships (Home Office, 2003a).

● The benefits given in points 1, 3 and 4 in the box are also identified by the National Audit Office in its report *Getting Citizens Involved: Community Participation in Neighbourhood Renewal* published in 2004 (National Audit Office, 2004).

● Additional benefits listed under points 6 and 7 were also identified by HM Treasury's cross-cutting review of the role of the voluntary and community sector (HM Treasury, 2002) and in its further publication in 2005 (HM Treasury, 2005).

Eight good reasons for community engagement

1 Taking on board a wide range of needs enables organisations to make better decisions about policy and services. It contributes to evidence-based policy making and enables organisations and partnerships to plan and provide services and programmes which more accurately meet need. In other words, it will lead to more *effective services* and programme implementation.

2 Services and programmes based on experience and knowledge drawn from communities are more likely to have community support. In other words, it will create greater *legitimacy* and credibility.

3 Projects or programmes developed on the basis of extensive community involvement are more likely to be sustainable over the longer term. In other words it will achieve greater *lasting impact* of effort and investment.

4 Active involvement helps to increase skill levels and build the confidence of communities. In other words it can be seen as part of a broader agenda of *building capacity*.

5 It encourages people to be more actively involved in the democratic process between elections. In other words, it addresses issues of *civil renewal* and the democratic deficit.

6 It can generate additional resource availability to complement services by involving volunteer and voluntary effort, through both individual and group activities. In other words, it will increase the *availability of resources*.

7 The voluntary and community sectors can add value to service delivery over and above those provided by the public sector, such as the ability to provide specialist services, deliver innovative approaches and engage with excluded groups. In other words it will give *added value*.

8 People have a right to influence decisions that affect their services, group or neighbourhood. In other words it will *address rights*.

From the point of view of the hard-nosed, over-worked service manager in a public sector agency, reasons 1 and 7 seem the most convincing. However, he or she may well say, *reasons* are not the same as *evidence*. Fortunately, several pieces of research do provide hard evidence for the positive impact of community engagement on services and programmes. Four recent key reports that are worth using and which provide evidence to justify the reasons are listed in the box opposite.

As an agency, since we organised better consultations
on the estate, we get shouted at less in the shops

The evidence

- *The Benefits of Community Engagement* – a review of the evidence commissioned by the Home Office and published July 2004. This looks at research on crime, health, regeneration, housing, employment and local government (Home Office, 2004d).

- *What Works in Community Involvement in Area-Based Initiatives?* – a review of the literature commissioned by the Home Office providing a useful critical examination based on a large number of studies (Home Office, 2004e).

- *Civic Renewal and Participation in Britain* – explores what we know about participation and its affects on policy making. Research commissioned by the Home Office, using the citizens' audit and census; includes some interesting material on the link between participation and reduced crime (Whiteley, 2004).

- *An Evaluation of Community Engagement in Achieving Sustainable Development in England* – interesting review of the impact of 18 rural-based projects, commissioned by the Department for Environment, Food and Rural Affairs (DEFRA) (DEFRA, 2004).

The model of community engagement

So what does engagement mean in practice? There seems to be a wide range of possibilities. Diagram 5, overleaf, contains a model that summarises a wide variety of forms of engagement available. The model is adapted from a community engagement template produced by a working group for the Home Office in 2004. As shown:

- Communities have six main options or routes for engagement.

- Public sector organisations – called agencies – have the same six options.

- The model suggests that both communities and the public sector need to contribute for effective engagement to happen – it cannot be one way.

- Both agencies and communities have the option of joint working with each other.

- Both agencies and communities have the option of supporting capacity building, which needs to underlie and strengthen all the other options.

Diagram 5 below also gives some examples under the options. Each option is now described in more detail.

Diagram 5: *The community engagement model*

CAPACITY BUILDING

COMMUNITY OPTIONS					AGENCY OPTIONS			
Organise community action	Provide community-led services	Individual citizen activity	Participate in community influence	Work jointly	Support community influence	Support individual activity	Support community-led services	Support community action
Local projects to tackle problems and needs	Directly providing formal services at neighbourhood, community of interest or district level	Formal volunteering through agencies	Groups responding to consultation and involvement opportunities	VCOs and public sector organisations jointly running services, projects and programmes	Organising consultation and involvement to influence services and programmes	Using and supporting formal volunteers	Commissioning services from voluntary and community organisations	Funding groups, projects and centres
Campaigns to obtain better services and more resources	Providing informal services – provided by community groups and centres	Formal volunteering through voluntary and community organisations (VCOs)	Selecting, electing and supporting representatives	Working in partnerships and involving community representatives	Developing effective channels for consultation	Using and supporting informal volunteering	Funding provision of informal services provided by community groups and centres	Responding to campaigns
Initiatives to challenge racism and discrimination		Informal volunteering for neighbours or local groups	Collectively influencing decisions on design and delivery of services and programmes	Forming compacts, agreements and community-based strategies	Responding to consultation and modifying practice as a result	Promoting staff volunteering where appropriate	Funding activities and the provision of informal services based in groups, projects or centres	Supporting initiatives to challenge racism and discrimination
		Key individual initiatives						

Community options – what communities can do

Organise community action

This can involve, for example, groups and networks organising their own self-help activities, running their own centres, and getting local people involved in practical initiatives to improve the environment. Community action is very much about communities doing things for themselves. It may also include groups organising campaigns to present the case for better services and increased resources.

Provide community-led services

For community sector groups and networks, this may mean taking on contracts to deliver services but more commonly involves providing what can be called 'informal services' such as a club run by a community centre. Such centres and informal services may be run on a purely voluntary basis and include activities that are not provided through funding from an external agency. Many such centres, for example, run youth activities or luncheon clubs for older people, based on voluntary help.

Individual citizen activity

This is about people being active in their communities in collective activities, such as formal volunteering through agencies. It can also involve volunteering through a voluntary or community organisation or informal volunteering, where the person helps out but without being supported or monitored by any organisation. It can also include individual initiatives, such as a one-person clean up of a site. Citizen activity means actions that in some ways benefit the community rather only the individual. It does not mean activities carried out purely for individual benefit or financial gain.

Participate in community influence

This is about *having a say* – local groups, active citizens, communities of interest and networks responding to consultation and involvement opportunities, and networks selecting or electing representatives to join a public sector management body or partnership. It is also about influencing decisions on the design and delivery of services and programmes. This is explored further below.

Agency options – what public sector organisations can do

Support community influence

This concerns decision-making. It includes organising systems, activities and events for consultation and involvement so that people and groups can influence the design and delivery of services and programmes. It could also involve changing the way the agency is organised and developing effective channels for consultation, for example by setting up and servicing an equalities forum. It could mean training community representatives in communication skills. It includes responding to groups and networks where they are involved in their own advocacy and campaigning. It could mean being proactive to organise community involvement rather than waiting until it happens! In total it means responding to and encouraging community influence and modifying practice and policy as a result.

Support individual activity

This could involve public sector organisations using volunteers as part of their service provision and ensuring their proper support and skill development in the process. It could mean supporting informal volunteering, for example, by helping a community centre train its army of unpaid helpers. It could mean organising the agency staff to act as volunteers for community projects. Such support always needs careful consideration of when it is appropriate to use a volunteer as opposed to a paid worker.

Support community-led services

This could involve a public sector body in commissioning services from voluntary and community organisations; it may mean directly funding groups, projects or centres. It could also involve funding the provision of informal services based in groups, projects or centres.

Support community action

This could include grant aid to groups, projects and centres. It could mean resourcing activities based in groups, projects or centres. It could mean supporting groups in practical and professional ways where they are taking their own initiatives but without dominating the process. It may involve responding to campaigns and advocacy.

What both agencies and communities can do

Work jointly

In this option, community organisations and agencies work together in designing and running services, projects and programmes. This involves a higher degree of engagement than community influence. It includes community organisations taking an active role, working in area-based and strategic partnerships to run projects and programmes jointly. It could include a number of groups and agencies coming together to form compacts, local area agreements and community-based strategies. Work jointly is explored further below.

Capacity building

In Diagram 5, capacity building is placed visually underlying the other options. This is because as a key option it needs to support and strengthen all the other available options. Expanding community-led services, for example, may require certain community and voluntary organisations to enhance their management abilities. Equally a public sector organisation may want to develop its staff's abilities to engage with community groups. It may want to develop the organisation's decision-making systems to be able to involve voluntary and community sector representatives more effectively. In other words, both voluntary and community organisations and public sector organisations may need to look at their development needs in order to be an effective part of community engagement. The model encourages a broad approach to capacity building, involving different sectors.

Using the community engagement model

- The model is useful to demonstrate that there is a wide range of options to consider in engagement processes. In particular, it shows that consultation, often wrongly regarded as all engagement is about, is only one of many options for the public sector.

- It shows that each element of community engagement has two sides to the coin – the options on each side are mirrored. This reflects the simple point that engagement needs to involve both the VCS and the public sectors to be effective. Consequently any strategy on engagement will need to consider both these aspects.

- The model is a spectrum, not a ladder. There is no assumption that any one element is better than any other. The most appropriate options will vary in each case, depending on the needs and resources of the community and the agency.

- The model does not imply that co-operation between sectors is always present. In some cases campaigning may be necessary and be an important pathway for some groups.

- Working jointly is an option. It implies a closer relationship than the other options. Working jointly will generally require increased capacity on behalf of both community and public sector participants. Recognition of this and its resource implications needs to be taken on board when considering which options to get involved in.

- Capacity building is an option. The model is useful to show the quite simple point that, for an agency, supporting capacity building is different from consulting community groups or working jointly with them. If an agency chooses to get involved in providing or funding community capacity building, for example, it would then form part of the *support organisations* as described in Chapter Four.

- The model presents both agencies and the community and voluntary sectors with the same set of options. Given that agencies generally have more resources, the model helps to indicate the pressures communities and their representatives can be under. It suggests that effective community engagement strategies adopted by agencies will need to bear this inequality in mind and allocate resources to address it.

The community engagement model can be used as a planning tool by voluntary and community sector organisations and by agencies to:

- identify the existing engagement options they are using and/or supporting

- identify gaps that may need addressing

- develop a plan to broaden or strengthen options

- use it to look at their own organisation's capacity building needs.

For one example see the box below. The model could also be used to assess the nature of community engagement at local or district level.

Ideally all the options will be looked at in any one neighbourhood or district. In the original concept from which the model was adapted, all parts of the model were expected to be put in place in order to achieve community engagement. Here however the model is not expected to be applied in every setting but is presented more as a checklist that can assist in developing a more informed and systematic approach to engagement. In some settings additional options may be needed to adapt the model for that specific context.

EXAMPLE

Using the community engagement model

A public sector organisation could:

- start by identifying which of the options it is already involved in and how. This would involve stocktaking and looking at the pattern of activity across the range of options

- assess if there are gaps. In identifying gaps there is a need to ask why this is and whether the gap needs addressing

- develop an action plan or strategy – if particular options need to be enhanced

- implement the action plan, which may involve the agency in its own capacity building activities, such as staff development or organisational changes. This can be called agency capacity building and can make use of the same four themes or building blocks introduced earlier. Agency capacity building is explored more later.

We believe the community engagement model is a major planning tool because it is compre-hensive – it relates to both communities and agencies – and because it shows capacity building as supporting all the options.

We now look in more detail at some of the issues for *public sector organisations* concerning two of the options – community influence and joint working. This is a brief summary, with signposting to further resources and information.

Community influence

An option on both sides of the community engagement model concerns community influence. For public sector organisations, supporting community influence includes many diverse activities and practices such as:

● consultation and involvement to influence the design and delivery of services and programmes

● developing effective channels for consultation

● responding to community influence and modifying practice as a result.

Supporting such influence from the community can be seen to involve at least three levels of participation (based on Wilcox, 1994). These levels provide useful insights:

● **Information giving** is the most basic starting point – communities cannot influence decision-making unless they know what is going on and what choices are available. *Information giving* underpins all other levels of participation, and may be appropriate on its own in some circumstances. The information-giving stance is essentially a 'take it or leave it' approach. However, you are likely to encounter problems if all you offer is information and people are expecting more involvement.

● **Consulting** – involves asking for views and perceptions on problems, issues and needs. *Consulting* may usually involve offering some options, allowing comment, taking account and then proceeding – perhaps after negotiation. The key point is that help in taking action is not being asked for – it is different from joint working. Consultation is appropriate when you can offer people some choices on what you are going to do – but is not the same as giving people the opportunity to develop their own ideas or participate in putting plans into action.

● **Deciding together** means being open to other people's ideas, and then choosing together from the range of options you have developed jointly. The basics of consultation apply, plus the need to generate ideas together, choose between them, and agree ways forward. *Deciding together* can be a more difficult stance from asking for views because it can mean giving people the power to choose, without them fully sharing the responsibility for carrying decisions through.

Agencies often confuse these three potential levels of influence and enter the arena without being clear about the stance they have chosen – or even thinking that there is a difference! In contrast, *working jointly* is a further step and involves more time and resources. It goes beyond making or influencing decisions, and is more about action.

How not to organise community consultations ...

If you really want to mess things up here's a useful checklist.

- Be unclear as to the aims and scope of the consultation.
- Initiate it too late to allow meaningful contributions or effectively inform decision-making.
- Use as much jargon as possible in the publicity material.
- Discuss it for ages in your own organisation first so there's no real options left.
- Involve only a limited range of people and organisations.
- If possible use inaccessible venues and don't offer help with child care.
- Organise the events to clash with religious holidays.
- Don't share what background information you have and don't say what the budget is.
- Just try selling the option you want anyway.
- When consulting, offer some ambitious options which definitely can't be afforded.
- Only listen to the usual suspects and those who shout loudest.
- Don't co-ordinate between agencies involved in similar events – try to duplicate if you can.
- Ensure the findings are not disseminated to participants.
- Try to ignore the conclusions and do what you would have done any way.
- Complete your monitoring form by ticking the box for effective consultations ...

To get to the meeting I had to search down the back of the sofa to see if I could find some cash – otherwise I just couldn't afford to get there

Joint working

Joint working between the VCS and public sector bodies is a key aspect of effective community engagement – as you can see from Diagram 5 it takes centre stage. Joint working may involve short-term collaboration or forming more permanent partnerships and agreements. Joint working in partnership involves both deciding together and acting together – it is usually more demanding on all parties involved. This means ideally having a common language, a shared vision of what you want, and the means to carry it out. To act together effectively, partners need to trust each other as well as agree on what they want to do. Each partner needs to feel they have an appropriate stake in the partnership and a fair say in what happens. Well, that's the ideal ...

Professionals and managers in public sector organisations sometimes have a number of negative perceptions about joint working. These can act as a block to achieving good practice and cultural change. These perceptions can be summed up in a number of pithy statements, as given in the box below. Interestingly, the same list of concerns can be heard spoken by VCS representatives about working with the public sector!

So as shown, the community engagement model can be of use to both VCS organisations and public sector agencies. We now explore how agencies can look at their own capacity building.

EXAMPLE

Blyth Valley Borough Council's approach to community engagement

This example shows a local authority that has taken a systematic approach to integrating community engagement into its culture and organisation.

Achieving the Council's vision of creating a cross-sector culture of community engagement involved three key outcomes:

- *Building community capacity* – this included creating a community development team and training a wider set of professionals in the community development approach, investing resources to develop a 'hub and spoke' network of community centres as community-led training venues.

- *Creating new forms of governance* – this included creating three community assemblies with delegated budgets linked to a neighbourhood management initiative to enable community influence at ward level on how services are delivered. Representatives from the community assemblies sit on the local strategic partnership.

- *Developing the community's ability to improve public services and do things for itself* – the voluntary and community sectors have been strengthened, with facilitation for the growth of infrastructure organisations that support other community and voluntary groups; new 'arm's length' companies that provide services have been encouraged as well as community work support to help establish a network of locally run training centres.

Community work input has focused on the areas with the highest levels of deprivation, where little or no community activity took place. In particular, the Council's approach to addressing the highly publicised drugs problem within Blyth Valley was to involve drug users to advise and help generate and deliver solutions. This approach has proved successful in reducing the level of drug related deaths and improving co-ordination between the services.

Fears about working jointly

- It will take too long and cost too much.
- They won't understand.
- They will only be interested in their own needs.
- We already know what they will say.
- They are too busy and we are too busy.
- They need to develop their communication skills.
- It will only be the usual suspects.
- Who do they represent anyway?
- We want to get on with delivering services, not talking about it.
- They want to hold on to their power and resources.

A ladder of participation

A widely quoted work on participation comes from Arnstein who suggested it could be described as a ladder with eight levels (Arnstein, 1971). A much more usable version of a 'ladder of participation' has been developed by Wilcox in *The Guidelines to Effective Participation* (1994). The three levels of information giving, consulting and deciding together described above, page 70 are the first three rungs of a ladder. The Wilcox ladder of participation also includes two further rungs of acting together where communities and agencies not only decide together but also work together and share responsibility. This is similar to joint working described here. The top rung is called supporting independent action which he describes as agencies helping others to develop and carry out their own plans. The ladder of participation is very useful as a planning tool; however the first three rungs tend to focus only on the issue of community influence, rather than the other wider options for engagement given in the engagement model described here.

Improving practice in the public sector

In order to achieve more effective community engagement, many agencies are taking a look at their policies and practices. Many have developed innovative and creative approaches and there is much good practice to build on. There is an extensive literature available on how to improve community engagement, some of which is listed in Resource Seven. The aim here is not to go into practical details but to give an overall framework that can be used by public sector agencies to improve policy and practice in engagement. This framework will be useful no matter which option or set of options is used from the community engagement model.

So what needs improving? For public sector organisations, this question can be looked at under the four headings introduced earlier.

Building skills

This can be seen as areas of professional development – for example, front-line staff and managers involved in engagement work may not have the skills and knowledge needed; staff may not know enough about communities of interest and their needs.

Building organisations

This can be seen as organisational change in the agency – for example, decision-making structures may not be designed for effective participation; there is inadequate provision of resources for consultation processes; there is a lack of appropriate consultation and feedback systems in the organisation; there is lack of a strategy on partnership working and participation; lack of leadership commitment to effective engagement processes.

Building involvement

This can be focused on tackling barriers – for example, meetings, events and communication may be organised in ways that alienate people; procedures, language and attitudes maintain the status quo.

Building equality

This can focus on addressing inequalities – for example, participation methods and processes may only focus on geographically-based communities, only involve larger voluntary organisations or a minority of representatives who are more confident and connected; there is a lack of effective contact and participation with communities of interest and excluded groups.

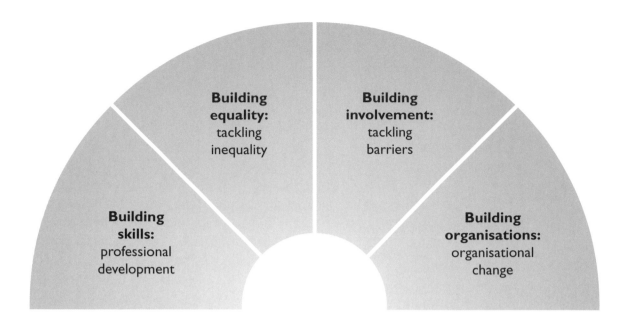

Building equality: tackling inequality

Building involvement: tackling barriers

Building skills: professional development

Building organisations: organisational change

Diagram 6: *Enhancing community engagement: four themes for supporting change in public sector organisations*

Each of these four headings is now looked at in turn, applied to public sector agencies. In combination, these four headings provide a framework for improving community engagement practices: see Diagram 6 above for a visual description. They provide a framework rather than a detailed tool kit, but draw on a number of practical sets of guidelines and tool kits listed in Resource Seven.

Agency capacity building

In working to enhance their engagement policy and practice, public sector organisations and partnerships can be seen to be involved in a form of capacity building, focusing on their own organisation. This can be described as *agency capacity building* and can be defined as:

> *Learning, resources and organisational change that increases the ability of public sector organisations to engage with communities effectively.*

The term *agency* is used here as shorthand to mean a range of public sector bodies, including for example, local authorities, primary care trusts, government offices, departments and universities. In this context, the aim of *agency capacity building* is to improve community engagement. Capacity building, including organisational development in agencies in its broad sense, can have a wide range of objectives, often linked to the corporate aims of the organisation. In order to remain focused, in this publication we limit the discussion concerning capacity building in agencies to improved practice and policy in community engagement.

Within the community engagement model, capacity building is shown to support all the other options. This means agencies may wish to look at their development needs in terms of enhancing their policies and practice in community engagement. *Agency capacity building* consequently can be a part of the application of the model.

University of Huddersfield's approach to community engagement

Many universities are involved in a variety of initiatives both to widen participation and to engage with communities. This example, from West Yorkshire, demonstrates a particular approach to organising engagement.

In Huddersfield the University was established in the early 1990s, and has close links with the area's traditional textile industries. Widening participation is organised using an 'embedded' approach with a small dedicated central widening participation (WP) office supporting each school to develop its own programmes of outreach and community-based education. This includes, for example, 'science communicators' who work with local schools to popularise science and a lively programme of art and design projects in museums and community centres. Students themselves use their placements to work with community groups including, for example, a website design project based in computing and engineering. The student union is proactive in opening up its own building for community use and seeing the student population as a volunteering resource. The WP office also works directly with community groups to build capacity in the district, for example using neighbourhood renewal funding to support community arts and festivals. This range of activity is co-ordinated by the external relations group and underpinned by a policy on involvement. The policy covers a range of practical and institutional issues as well as outlining the expectations placed upon both the University and its staff on the one hand and the voluntary and community sectors on the other.

Building skills: professional development

Building skills, in this context, concerns skills, experience, knowledge, behaviours and confidence needed in agencies for effective engagement. Building skills for professional development can involve staff and officers at a number of levels in the organisation:

- community workers and practitioners who work directly with users, volunteers, community groups and networks

- other front-line staff who relate directly to communities through providing services – including, for example, police officers, teachers, health professionals, academics and business advisors

- managers who are based in service provision and are involved in consulting and engaging with community groups, representatives and networks

- senior managers and policy officers who oversee and resource community engagement activities

The Learning Curve, produced as part of the neighbourhood renewal strategy, gives a useful description of the professional skills needed for effective engagement (ODPM, 2002). Many staff already have lots to build on and share, especially where they are trained in community work. Professional development to develop such skills, where needed, can be supported in a number of ways. Human resources departments will need to take a key role in this, with backing from senior managers. Examples are:

- introductory courses on community engagement and understanding the community and voluntary sectors

- short training courses in specific practical skill areas, such as consultation methods

- placements for staff with community and voluntary organisations

- training in core community work skills for practitioners and councillors

- community development input at policy and practice levels for managers and policy-makers

- learning sets can involve staff from different departments and backgrounds

- networks can be established as learning forums involving staff from other agencies and people from the VCS

- experienced residents and community organisers acting as mentors and trainers.

The specific knowledge, skills and behaviours needed to enhance community engagement can be included in professional competences that inform job descriptions and personnel specifications. Community work as a professional discipline has now been fully described as a set of occupational standards which can contribute to this. For further information on community work see Resource Six.

EXAMPLE

The Learning Curve in Sandwell, West Midlands

The Sandwell Partnership has produced its own local version of the Learning Curve. It uses a stakeholder approach, defining stakeholders as 'those, whether individuals or organisations, who have a direct interest in the success of the regeneration and neighbourhood renewal agenda'. It outlines a comprehensive strategy to increase skills and knowledge for effective regeneration, including practitioners, professionals, policy-makers, residents and organisations. It uses the different starting points of stakeholders, valuing their different contributions and acknowledging they will have varying needs.

The role of councillors

Members at parish, district and county levels have a key role to play in supporting and participating in professional development programmes. Their understanding of its role from their work with communities is helpful to give authorities' officers the policy-level backing to develop their skills and organise capacity building programmes for council staff. They have a wealth of experience in community engagement and can act in an advisory role for how programmes are designed and developed. Equally, many members are themselves requesting training and support in order to strengthen their own skills and knowledge of working in and with community and voluntary groups. Many members not directly involved in a council executive or 'cabinet' have further developed their roles as 'enablers' to help voluntary and community groups to be better organised and better resourced. They can also play an invaluable role in mentoring community groups to help them gain the skills and confidence in dealing with officers in meetings.

EXAMPLE

Professional development in Bradford District

In Bradford District, Bradford Vision, the local strategic partnership, and the local authority have led on setting up an inter-agency training programme on consultation and participation skills. The programme is aimed at public sector employees who carry out or plan consultation with service users. It consists of ten short modules covering themes such as hard to reach groups, public meetings, research, focus groups, planning for real and questionnaire design. There is a core module that all participants need to go on before proceeding with other more specific modules. Flexible timing, accessible venues and absence of charges have all contributed to the programme being very popular and repeated due to demand.

Building organisations: organisational change

This is the second of the four themes that can be used help to improve engagement practices. In this context, building organisations concerns *organisational change* that is to do with how the organisation relates to communities. It means putting in place structures and systems that will enhance effective engagement and the ability to respond to new information, priorities and needs (Smithies and Webster, 1998). The changes may mean, for example:

- a hard look at structures and systems, in particular concerning decision-making

- delegating some decision-making to an area or community level

- setting up a lead 'champion' senior manager and, if a local authority, a political lead role for engagement

- establishing a strategy on community engagement with an effective resource to achieve it

- ensuring effective communication with the voluntary and community sectors is developed and reviewed

- setting community involvement objectives for appropriate units and teams

- building performance indicators on community engagement into service delivery targets

- establishing specialist teams of community development and capacity building workers

- ensuring the organisation's research function includes gathering data on community engagement needs.

Organisational change ideally needs to involve a number of levels simultaneously within the agency – from the individual staff member to the team, unit, section, department and executive body. In particular it requires commitment at the most senior level to be effective. It needs an overview at senior management level to co-ordinate not just what is being developed and changed but also how it is being changed (Smithies and Webster, 1998). Systems may need to be developed to cater for consultation cycles and will need officer support. For example, the Cabinet Office recommends that government departments use a consultation co-ordinator to assess effectiveness and monitor progress.

- Some local authorities have established special forums to consult with communities of interest. For such initiatives to work requires high-level political backing and skilful outreach work.

- Some local authorities are decentralising the budgetary decision-making processes to area-based committees, in particular for more visible services such as cleansing. Such initiatives have a long history in local government and need careful planning to avoid past problems.

- Some primary care trusts have established a senior management post specifically to lead on community engagement.

- Some universities have adopted community engagement strategies.

EXAMPLE

Organisational change in Blyth Valley Borough Council

The Council restructured in 2001 to reinforce the importance of community leadership as its core role. Political responsibility has been identified through the allocation of portfolio responsibilities, with the leader taking direct responsibility for community involvement and development. This is with the support of the executive director with cross-cutting responsibilities for driving community engagement throughout the authority. Corporate and service strategies are aligned to community development goals and key staff have been trained in the principles of community development, with the role of cascading that knowledge throughout the organisation and within wider partnerships.

Building involvement: tackling barriers

Building involvement in this context involves tackling barriers that reduce the effective participation of communities in agencies. This will vary depending on the organisation and the setting. Obviously some of the issues in enhancing community involvement have already been identified in *building skills* and *building organisations* looked at so far, but here the theme of barriers to involvement is looked at as a key focus and is taken further. Here's a checklist that can be useful as a prompt.

- *Physical:* Buildings used by public agencies for meetings and consultation events may not be fully accessible, or may be viewed locally as limited to certain groups or clans. Transport problems can alienate some people from participating, especially in rural areas.

- *Timing:* In many cases, a 12-week consultation period for community groups will be needed. This is especially important for grass-roots groups, which are often at the end of the communication chain and not immediately a part of the voluntary sector mainstream arena.

- *Resources:* Involving groups, leaders and networks in *community influence* and *joint working* will require resources, for example, for venues and access. This needs to be catered for adequately in budgets.

- *Culture:* The culture of an organisation consists partly of attitudes and perceptions: for example officers and councillors in a local authority may often be used to acting *for* the community, rather than working *with* it. Working *with* will require changes, based on a new understanding of the relationship (Gaventa, 2004). This could involve new knowledge and skills to understand the roles of democratic leadership in relation to community representation.

- *Outreach:* The role of outreach is often not understood by agencies. Involving communities of interest, for example, may mean working with networks which are at a relatively low level of organisation compared with other neighbourhood-based groups. This will involve using community development practitioners with the appropriate skills and experience and giving time for such contact and relationship building to be carried out.

- *Political:* The term political is used here in a general sense to mean the use of power. Despite having grand policy statements and staff skilful in engagement practices, some public sector organisations, when it comes down to it, maintain their power over decision-making at the executive level. ODPM explores these issues in *Why Neighbourhoods Matter*, a publication that promotes greater decentralisation in local authority decision-making (ODPM, 2005a).

A useful analysis of different conceptions of power and the implications for participation and empowerment is given in *Public Policy in the Community* (Taylor, 2003). A number of theories are examined that describe how policy-making occurs, with different implications on how communities can access power processes.

As well as doing outreach work,
we need to do inreach – opening up our agency
to real engagement

A review of engagement and ways forward

In a broad-ranging review under the theme of governance, Gaventa traces many similar trends in Western European countries, the US and in the Developing World. The relationship between the governed and government is becoming blurred – the traditional pattern of elected representatives, supported by an expertise-based bureaucracy, making decisions then communicated to a passive electorate, is increasingly being enhanced by more direct forms of engagement. Gaventa's research published by ODPM in 2004 concluded with some key proposals for improving community engagement:

- **A public commitment** from agencies to effective community engagement needs to be made in a policy statement, shared by the main players in the public, voluntary and community sectors at district level, ideally based in the local strategic partnership. In some cases such a commitment can be expressed through a compact or strategy on engagement, as discussed below. The key issue is that it is a public statement that has political backing in the widest sense of the word.

- **Guidelines** are needed which clarify the appropriate roles and rules for engagement between elected representatives, officers and community leaders relating to local strategic partnerships and local authorities. These need also to 'clarify the different forms of accountability which underlie different forms of representation'.

- **The legislative framework** for incorporating participation in local governance needs to be changed in order to incorporate more effective forms of participation and representation with elected leaders. This would include approaches to planning at local government level that link community representatives and elected council members in joint forms of decision-making. It would also establish a legislative basis for more popular and direct forms of participation at the local level, drawing extensively on experiences from Developing World settings (Gaventa, 2004).

Building equality: tackling inequalities

Building equality concerns *tackling inequalities* and is the fourth theme on improving policy and practice in community engagement. Many agencies are committed to ensuring engagement is based on equality principles and there is a lot of good practice to build on. This section does not offer a ready-made 'one size fits all' way forward but a checklist to act as a prompt that can be adapted depending on particular organisational needs. The term *equality* as suggested in Chapter Four can be divided into headings. Many of the same or similar issues apply:

Equal opportunities

- Are all sections of communities given equal chance to get involved, be consulted and work jointly?

- Has a mapping exercise been carried out to identify the range of groups and cultures in the community?

- Are the needs of communities of interest considered in engagement processes?

- Does an emphasis on neighbourhood-based involvement in effect exclude those people who identify more with groups spread across the district?

- Is capacity building available to all local groups or are some such as Eastern European groups excluded?

- Has the organisation of capacity building considered access issues in all its forms?

Diversity

- Are faith groups recognised as a part of the community and voluntary sectors?

- Is language support provided where needed?

- Does the way information is communicated cater for different needs?

- Do decision-making arrangements reflect the make up of the range of communities?

- Does the way engagement activities are organised show sensitivity to the cultural and religious needs of black and minority ethnic communities?

- Are conflicts of needs recognised and support available to deal with them?

- Is the diversity of communities reflected in the background of staff involved in organising engagement activities?

- Does the monitoring of engagement processes consider diversity issues?

Links

This is about how well connected communities and groups are and how engagement processes can build links that bring people together.

- Does engagement increase understanding and tolerance between different sections in communities?

- Does engagement reduce conflict and tensions – or worsen them?

- Does engagement encourage contact and communication between different cultures and communities?

- Does engagement encourage larger voluntary and community organisations to support smaller or more marginalised ones?

- Does engagement help to build community and professional networks that include everyone interested?

- Do engagement activities bring people together– and if not why?

Using the four themes

Using the four themes of *building skills, organisations, involvement* and *equality* is one way of improving policy and practice in engagement. There are many other useful frameworks available on the subject, as well as practical tool kits which broadly serve the same purpose, each of which has a particular setting and aim. The key difference here is that these four themes directly relate to the four building blocks developed in Chapter Four. This mirroring of themes applied both to community capacity building and to public sector-based engagement is intentional. It means that at community level and in large organisations, the same questions can be asked and in many cases – where appropriate – looked at jointly. The art of doing this and using the four blocks in this dual way is discussed in Chapter Six. This dual use of the community engagement model – by both VCS and agencies – is intentional in order to encourage the view that capacity building is equally important in public sector organisations as it is in the voluntary and community sectors.

EXAMPLE

The four building blocks in Bradford District

The use of the four building blocks for capacity building both at community level and in agencies was developed in Bradford District by the Building Communities Partnership. The four themes were originally adapted from an evaluation system called Achieving Better Community Development which has been widely used across Britain. In Bradford the four themes were the basis of extensive discussion on community engagement, involving over two hundred community and voluntary organisations and groups. It led to the Building Communities Strategy 2000–05 which involved objectives and targets for both the VCS and for agencies. This joint approach to capacity building helped to inspire this book!

Community engagement and strong communities

A description of what a *strong community* might look like was given in Chapter Two. It can be summed up as one that is active, participative, organised, accepting, connected and fair. Working towards achieving those six qualities in full strength will involve the participation of many agencies, partnerships and the local authority. Community engagement activities and initiatives can all contribute to achieving *strong communities* as well as the contribution that community capacity building will make. The four themes explored in this Chapter will help to identify the changes needed in agencies so that they can contribute to strengthening communities.

This Chapter has explored the link between capacity building and community engagement. The community engagement model clearly demonstrates that capacity building needs to inform all the options needed for effective practice. As a model, it also firmly places capacity building in both agencies and communities – a dual approach that challenges the assumption that capacity building is mainly needed to address community level needs.

We now move on in Chapter Six to look at what a strategic approach to capacity building can mean.

The Story

The meeting went badly, at least at first. In the initial chat it seemed to Dave, Jimmy and the others on the Executive that Ms Patel seemed rather stuck on the idea that all Social Services wanted to do was to consult in future with the MS Action Group and that was about it. She seemed rather defensive – wasn't that what they wanted – a say about services for MS 'sufferers'? Wasn't that what community engagement was all about? From her perspective, the 'Executive' seemed quite agitated – they obviously had different ideas. It was a tense moment – were they all going to blow up about it?

'Can I just give an outline of what we do and what we'd like to do?' David seemed the calmest of the gang, and obviously had a good picture of what was needed. She was happy to listen to him. 'Firstly there is the centre we run here – all with voluntary input from our members offering advice, support and counselling. For people with MS all that's important – people are often going through a crisis in their image of themselves and need a lot of help – I did. We also provide volunteers – about a hundred, spread out across the district to visit people in their own homes. And yes, we do run campaigns – last year Jimmy led on a benefits campaign that encouraged members to claim what was theirs by right, even though agencies had to be pressurised into accepting it. But we could do more, and we are not just a source of volunteers. We're ready now as a group, well, community organisation, with a constitution and accounts. We want to bid for a contract now from Social Services.'

Dave paused – he wanted it to go well. He was surprised how confident he had come across! Gita seemed more relaxed now and responded positively: 'Can you put this all in writing? It would be helpful for me – we are initiating a new strategy on what's called capacity building and I need some practical examples. You've obviously all come along way. Your course sounds interesting too. I could do with assertion training myself.'

Getting to know them during the meeting was quite an eye opener for Gita – all their stuff about people's patronising attitudes and the discrimination they felt about being labelled – it could have been her own family talking about their experience on the streets. It had ended well, an exchange of down to earth views and a promise from Gita to take their proposal, once properly prepared in writing, to the relevant council committee.

The way forward
– developing plans and strategies

To be effective, capacity building will need to be planned and organised carefully and based on certain principles. This will apply at every level, from working with one community group or project, a neighbourhood, community of interest, network, agency, partnership or across a whole district. This Chapter looks at ways of doing this and describes a ten point planning process.

The main arguments in Chapter Six are:

- capacity building needs to be planned rather than a response to short-term or specific needs

- the planning process has ten key elements

- the four building blocks of Building skills, Building organisations, Building involvement, and Building equality can form a useful part of the planning process

- a strategic approach is needed at district level to take a long-term view of capacity building.

Planning is needed to ensure that capacity building addresses real needs, is based on principles, and relates to the wider context of community engagement. It will be very limited in impact if it is a series of one-off uncoordinated activities and projects; capacity building needs planning to build a lasting impact. We start by describing the ten key planning elements, and then move on to discuss planning in specific settings of working with groups and in neighbourhoods. Most of this material relates to the community sector but is relevant to the wider context.

Ten key elements in the planning process

When planning capacity building, the ten main things to consider are:

- decide what it is for
- decide on the participants
- involve other partners
- assess needs and strengths
- clarify the objectives
- use the four building blocks
- identify resources and funding

- establish an evaluation method

- organise activities and programmes

- develop relationships.

In using these elements please note:

- These are not set stages to go through – in particular the first four elements need to be considered jointly. For example, it may be that a survey of needs indicates who the participants for the capacity building could be. Alternatively, identifying needs may require the prior involvement of partners.

- Not every element will apply to every situation or need. This Chapter gives a broad overview – adaptation to the particular setting will be needed in each case.

- Where we refer to capacity building in agencies, we limit discussion to capacity building in relation to enhanced community engagement, rather than the wider field of organisational development in the public sector.

- The planning system described here needs to be used creatively – in some cases responding to an opportunity may lead to initiatives that are not part of a wider planning process but are still very useful.

We now go through the ten planning points, and then look at planning issues with groups and in neighbourhoods.

The ten key planning elements

Decide what it is for

Decide on the participants

Involve other partners

Assess needs and strengths

Clarify the objectives

Use the four building blocks

Identify resources and funding

Establish an evaluation system

Organise activities and programmes

Develop relationships

Decide what it is for

Capacity building is a means to an end, not an end in itself. It is worth being clear early in the planning process about the *why* and to describe that as an impact or outcome. For example, the aim may be for:

- the gala to be well organised (community activity)

- the community centre to be well run (informal services)

- the housing improvements to address needs (formal services)

- groups of different backgrounds to get on better (cohesion).

The nature of the outcome will vary depending on the level:

- **local level** – it may be related to one group, event, centre or service

- **neighbourhood level** – it may be related to the development of the whole estate or area

- **strategic level** – it may be across a district, related to, for example, a housing policy or community strategy.

This initial discussion can help get the planning process started. There are questions, too, about who is involved and what needs will be addressed. Often after such further work on identifying needs and participants, it is useful to tighten up defining the objectives: this is discussed below on page 87.

Decide on the participants

A basic decision is: who are the participants for the capacity building? There are a number of options. The aim of the following checklist is to expand the range of possible choices and encourage joint planning.

- *Individuals* – active individuals in the community such as community representatives, volunteers, individual members of groups, local leaders and campaigners, community entrepreneurs; front-line staff, professionals and managers. Deciding this may involve prioritising particular groups such as women or people with disabilities.

- *Groups and projects* – such as a residents' or user group, community association, project or locally-run community centre.

- *The voluntary and community sectors' workforce* – staff and managers in community and voluntary organisations.

- *Networks* – a large number of groups or individual members.

- *A parish or village* – where based in a more rural environment.

- *Neighbourhood* – addressing the needs of a large number of local groups and geographically-based communities.

- *Communities of interest* – where a community may not be geographically based.

- *Programmes* – capacity building for effective implementation of a government programme at local level.

- *Partnerships* – specifically to build an effective partnership body.

- *Parish and local authority council members* – who may have their own specific capacity building needs.

- *Front-line public sector agency* – for example, staff who interact with community groups and networks.

- *Community development workers* – can be both paid and volunteer workers.

- *Public sector managers and policy officers* – especially those directly engaging with communities.

Considering the needs of the community and voluntary sectors' workforce and the regional or sub-regional level is also very important, though outside the scope of this book. The emphasis of this chapter is on *community capacity building*, though many of the points made will be equally useful with the whole of the voluntary and community sectors.

Making decisions on who the participants are could be informed by a number of factors; again these will vary between local level and strategic level planning. Here are some of the questions that could be considered, on which group or type of participants.

- Are they particularly in areas of stress and deprivation?

- Are they particularly in need of community capacity building?

- Are they asking for help?

- Do they have the greatest opportunities in terms of being linked to new projects or initiatives?

It may, for example, be that some community groups are requesting help with capacity building but are already relatively well organised and accessing services. Within the limited resources of any one project, programme or policy, hard decisions will need to be made to identify priorities.

Capacity building can't be forced on people – many groups are already under a lot of pressure

Involve other partners

Involving representatives from a range of organisations and sectors will be important. A stakeholder approach is useful here – that is, considering who may be involved in resourcing the inputs and organising the activities, and who will be affected by the outcomes of the capacity building. To identify stakeholders, it is useful to ask a series of questions.

- Who is likely to benefit?

- Who will be the participants?

- Who may be adversely affected?

- Who can help or hinder?

- Who may have the necessary skills and resources?

- Who is involved in the wider context of community engagement?

- Who leads on relevant action plans and strategies?

As suggested, planning is often more effective when different organisations consider their needs jointly. In some cases this may involve both voluntary and community sector groups and public agencies. A guiding principle is that the main sector that is the recipient of capacity building should take a lead role in its planning.

- Key partners could be organisations that provide *support* as discussed in Chapter Three and those in the voluntary and community sectors providing *infrastructure.*

- One way to involve partners is to base the planning in an existing local or strategic partnership. If so, the partnership will need to consider if it represents an effective spread of stakeholders.

- In some cases, it may be best to set up a new capacity building partnership or steering group that is dedicated to these issues.

- For small pieces of work and, in some cases, work locally with individuals and single groups, such elaborate partnership arrangements would not be appropriate.

In practice there is no neat starting point. Available funding or clearly defined targets may determine who the participants can be for capacity building, or a partnership already in existence may decide to survey local needs. The main point is that whatever your starting position, it is useful to consider carefully the questions concerning who are the *participants* and who are the *partners.*

Assess needs and strengths

This will sound obvious – but it is still overlooked: capacity building should be based on some form of assessing needs.

- The Active Citizens Framework, introduced in Resource Three, is a way of finding out about needs of active *individuals* and can be used to complement the planning process.

- Some approaches to identifying needs in community capacity building with *groups* are looked at in Resource Four.

- Needs and strengths can be identified under different headings. There are various ways this could be done. The four building blocks of building skills, building organisations, building involvement, and building equality can provide a useful set of headings, which are discussed below in this context.

The allocation of resources to capacity building provision on a district or local basis will ideally be based on an analysis of needs and strengths in relation to existing provision – that is, building a picture of what is needed in relation to existing capacity building support.

- Methods are available to assist in surveying and identifying the existing level of both needs and support, as discussed below (and see Resources 4 and 5).

- Ideally a baseline picture will be built up that describes the situation at the start of any particular capacity building support and activity, as appropriate to the scale of the initiative.

- It will not always be possible to carry out such robust information collection; however the effective planning of capacity building will need to give some consideration to the issue of existing needs in relation to existing provision, at least in a general manner.

Clarify the objectives

Deciding what the capacity building is for, as described above, is a general initial process to help get started with planning. Once more information on needs has been collected and there is a clearer idea of who is involved, it is worth writing a statement on the objectives of the capacity building in relation to the identified needs. The *objectives* can relate to four types of outcomes:

- *policy objectives,* such as improving services and creating stronger communities, as discussed in Chapter Two

- *sector objectives*, such as strengthening the voluntary and community sectors or particular parts of them, as discussed in Chapter Three

- *group objectives*, such as building the organisational abilities of groups, as discussed in Chapter Four

- *relationship objectives*, in terms of effective engagement, as discussed in Chapter Five.

Vague statements such as 'the aim of the project is to empower groups' or 'support the network' need more clarity and detail. A key finding of the Home Office's review of government departments (Home Office, 2004a) was that too often increased capacity is an assumed outcome or aspect of government programmes, without consciously directing resources to achieve the desired end.

In addition, the statement of objectives may need to be placed in a wider context of:

- existing plans that groups have involving capacity building

- existing neighbourhood action plans

- how it relates to any existing Change Up plan

- how it relates to the broader agenda of effective community engagement

- key strategies in the neighbourhood or district related to the development of communities, for example, the community strategy, adult learning, widening participation in higher education, neighbourhood renewal, community cohesion and economic regeneration.

Please don't feel overwhelmed! These are options – they may not be relevant in every case; the main thing is to be clear about what you want to achieve and who it directly relates to.

Use the four building blocks

The four blocks as discussed in Chapter Four can provide a framework for planning and organising capacity building that is useful in a variety of sectors and settings. As a reminder, the four blocks in community capacity building are:

- Building skills

- Building organisations

- Building involvement

- Building equality.

Applying the four blocks and the issues they raise for capacity building can act as a checklist to ensure key principles are being considered and acted upon. For each activity of *community capacity building*, the following can be asked.

- **Building skills:** How does it address skills?

- **Building organisation:** How does it build the community or voluntary organisation?

- **Building involvement:** How does it improve involvement?

- **Building equality:** How does it tackle issues of equality?

Here are two examples:

- **Groups** – a request has come from several groups in a neighbourhood for a learning input on management committee skills; working with the groups may bring out a wider range of needs concerning how they involve marginalised groups in the neighbourhood and their level of access to people with disabilities (*building skills and building equality*).

- **Networks** – a network may have a well-developed policy on involvement and equal opportunities and be inclusive in how it organises its meetings and events. Working with the network reveals a lack of an appropriate structure. In practice that means it is losing members and drifting from achieving its original aims (*building involvement and building organisations*).

The four blocks act as a prompt to take a wide view of the development of groups and networks. They have principles built into them, as discussed in Chapter Four.

As well as being useful in planning capacity building in community settings, the four themes can equally be used to strengthen community engagement policy and practice in agencies and partnerships. For this setting, the four building block headings have been adapted to suit the context – and language – of public sector organisations. For each activity of *agency capacity building* it can be asked:

- **Building skills:** How does this address professional development?

- **Building organisations:** How does this support organisational change?

- **Building involvement:** How does this tackle barriers?

- **Building equality:** How does this tackle issues of inequality?

For example:

- **Public sector agency** – a primary care trust (PCT) may have a written policy on community involvement and be organising a wide range of open meetings to consult local people in decision-making on its services. However, some professionals working in the PCT on community engagement express a need to develop their skills in relating to communities (*building skills*).

There are clearly links between the different themes in different sectors. Using the four themes in these different settings creates opportunities for joined-up thinking and planning. Here are two examples:

- **Public sector agency** – staff in the PCT through discussion with community networks jointly form a learning set involving both paid staff and community representatives (*building skills*).

- **Local strategic partnerships (LSPs)** – an LSP, while having community representatives on several of its partnerships and the main board, lacks any form of larger network to relate to in the district. The LSP begins work with existing infrastructure organisations in the voluntary and community sectors to help to consult on, and then with local backing, create a new community network (*building involvement*).

- **Infrastructure organisations** – several voluntary organisations that provide infrastructure services link with local agencies and the local authority to review their support work with groups on equality and diversity issues *(building equality)*.

As shown in these examples, the four building blocks can act as a useful framework to ensure different aspects of capacity and strengths are being looked at. The four building blocks planning model in Diagram 6 below shows how the four blocks can inform capacity building in both the voluntary and community sectors and in partnerships and public sector organisations.

A few key points about the use of the four blocks in planning capacity follow.

- Using all four will not always fit or be appropriate – for example, if working just with individual volunteers to look at their learning needs, organisational development may not be appropriate.

- The links between sectors may need to be addressed in stages – some groups may want to start with locally-based training but over time ask to link up with staff from a public agency.

- Joint capacity building between sectors may not always be useful or appropriate. However, as argued, the key thing is to be fully aware of the options and make informed choices.

- The VCS and its infrastructure organisations in particular can have a key role, that needs to be resourced properly, in helping to build the capacity of the public sector for effective engagement.

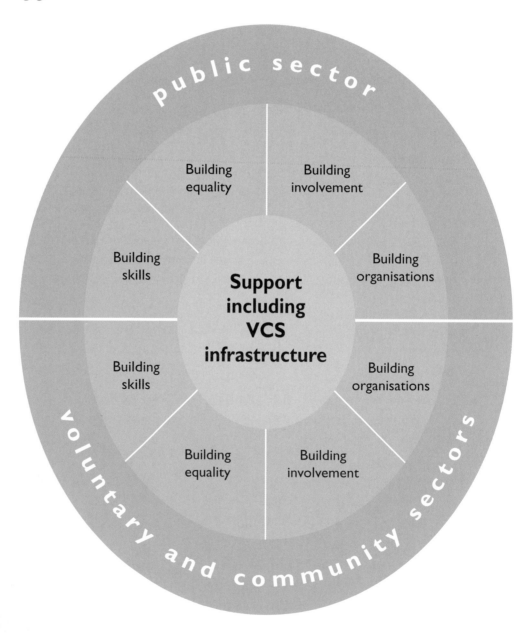

Diagram 6: *The four building blocks planning model*

Identify resources

Every particular capacity building initiative will have its own funding and resource opportunities and difficulties.

- Resources can include a wide range of forms of support, including finance, staff time, volunteer time, buildings, child care and transport – see Resource Five for further ideas.

- Resource needs may change over time. For example, the first year of a capacity building project may require research and incur setting-up costs.

- Some capacity building will need outreach work built into the resource budget for it to have real impact.

- The cost of evaluation, as appropriate to the scale of the capacity building programme or activity, needs to be considered from the start.

In terms of resources for community capacity building, key points concerning the national scene are:

- *Change Up* was launched in 2004 and the Active Communities Unit in the Home Office now leads on implementation. A budget of £80 million was earmarked up to March 2006 to support the strategy. In 2005 a further £70 million for 2006–08 was announced, with some changes to the delivery mechanisms, including a move to a sector-led delivery agency along the lines of Futurebuilders

- *Firm Foundations* was launched in 2004 but with no significant budget to support its development other than a relatively small fund to develop community mentoring

- *European Structural Funding* has been a key source of funding for certain forms of capacity building but will cease to operate in the same way in Britain from 2006

- the *neighbourhood renewal* strategy will finish its *current* round of funding in 2006; it is unclear yet on the future direction of the next round of funding and how much capacity building will be prioritised

- the *rural strategy* on community capacity building in England can be accessed through a key publication published in 2003 (DEFRA, 2003)

- *local area agreements* are likely to become major vehicles for channelling funding for capacity building

- *Working Together*, an initiative originating in the Learning and Skills Council, can be a source of financial support for community capacity building: see *Working Together*, overleaf.

Futurebuilders

Futurebuilders came from HM Treasury's cross-cutting review of the role of the voluntary and community sectors (HM Treasury, 2002). Futurebuilders consists of a fund directed at those organisations working in the fields of health and social care, crime, community cohesion, education and learning, and support for children and young people. The scheme only covers capital or non-recurrent revenue spending. Local strategic priorities will need to be taken into account when developing proposals for Futurebuilders funding. The national fund of £125 million over three years is not divided on a regional or district basis, nor is level of deprivation part of the allocation criteria. Consequently it is hard to predict the amount that comes to any district. The funding contains a substantial element of loan-based assistance. The commitment to repay loans, where income will need to be generated through future service delivery contracts, may alienate some potential participating organisations.

Working Together

This new strategy was published by the Learning and Skills Council (LSC) in May 2004 (LSC, 2004a). A key aim is for the LSC to take full advantage of the contribution that voluntary and community sector organisations can make to improve the access, range and quality of education and training provision for individuals, employers and the wider community. The strategy particularly focuses on a set of roles that the voluntary and community sector can play in its relationship with the LSC:

- as a provider of learning opportunities
- as an employer
- as a source of expertise and communication.

As a provider of learning opportunities, community and voluntary organisations can make a major contribution to community capacity building. In particular the LSC sees them as being able to access and involve marginalised groups in learning. The LSC's aim is to put this relationship on a proper footing, for example by increasing access to its mainstream budgets rather than only using project-based funding streams. This is also by ensuring full costs are catered for and by going for more stable, longer-term funding relationships. This initiative involves capacity building on two levels – for front-line community groups and individuals and also developing the capacity of the learning providers themselves to take on contracts and use the Common Inspection Framework. In addition to *Working Together*, the LSC in 2004 developed an adult learning category called *Learning for Active Citizenship and Community Development* (LSC, 2004b). This includes community-based learning developed with local residents to build the skills, knowledge and understanding needed for community participation and involvement, including those required for community action.

Establish an evaluation method

It is important to know what impact the capacity building is having. An evaluation and monitoring system will need to be set up early on rather than just being an afterthought at the end of the capacity building support. The evaluation of capacity building is still in its infancy as a discipline; a brief summary of existing methods and some of the issues involved is given in Resource Eight.

Organise activities and programmes

Activities here means training and learning opportunities, including a variety of forms of adult learning and informal education, tailored to the needs of members of groups and networks. The term *activities* also means the organisational development of groups and networks through advice and support, information, facilitation and consultancy. Resource Two contains further discussion of activities in community capacity building. Both learning and organisational change can be partly provided through mutual support and sharing between groups. A combination of activities over time organised in a planned manner can be called a *programme* of capacity building. Some points to note are:

- The process may need flexibility when working in community settings. Some groups, especially people who are marginalised and hard to reach, may need additional outreach and time to build relationships where active learning can take place. Building strengths can be developmental in that one set of activities can be built upon to develop new initiatives and outputs. The design of activities and programmes may need to cater for this flexibility and a build up in stages of greater levels of involvement by participants.

● Working in and with communities requires a particular skill-set on behalf of practitioners and professionals. These are described for example in *The Learning Curve* (ODPM, 2002). Civil servants involved in the design and administration of programmes will need a certain level of knowledge of community engagement and capacity building (see *The Learning Curve*). In particular, staff involved in delivery will need community work skills and experience; these can be described as a set of competences through the occupational standards in community development.

● In many cases, voluntary and community organisations can be commissioned to provide community capacity building provision; for local provision, the voluntary and community sector infrastructure can be seen as the most appropriate provider of activities. The advantages of such a role have been explored in the HM Treasury's cross-cutting review (HM Treasury, 2002). Local partnerships, with a brief to implement a governmental programme at local level, could involve infrastructure organisations as community capacity building providers on a grant or commissioning basis.

Develop relationships

Involving partners at an early stage, as discussed, is central to the effective planning of capacity building. In addition, building relationships on an on-going basis needs to be considered and worked on for many different reasons, such as to:

● develop an understanding of the role of capacity building

● maintain an information flow on problems and progress

● build widespread support for capacity building

● involve organisations in further outreach work for getting other people involved as participants

● prepare service managers for the increased community engagement

● obtain further funding and resources for further programmes and projects

● disseminate findings learnt from the evaluation to other districts and interested parties.

We prepared a well written plan with a lot of support but over time we lost contact with the original people involved including councillors; the plan suffered from a lack of funding as a result

As shown, the ten planning points provide a rough outline to the issues and processes involved in planning. They certainly do not cover everything and will not be applicable in every case but they are a basis to use and adapt as needed.

EXAMPLE

Developing relationships in Bradford

The neighbourhood renewal team within Bradford Vision, the local strategic partnership in Bradford District, regards developing relationships as a key part of its work. In particular this involves supporting public service providers in developing their planning systems. The aim of this is to integrate the findings from neighbourhood action plans drawn up by local communities and communities of interest. Developing relationships is also about helping residents and communities of interest to take a broader picture to regeneration where some are perhaps preoccupied with their own immediate issue or area. This has meant building the links between local small-scale changes in how services are delivered and the bigger picture of achieving real strategic changes across the district. This has used 'small steps to demonstrate success' as a key theme for building relationships.

Planning capacity building with one group

We now move on to look at the planning of capacity building in specific settings. An individual community group may wish to develop its own capacity building plan. This can be useful to:

- ensure capacity building within the organisation is clearly targeted to address needs and problems

- help obtain funding

- contribute to a neighbourhood plan or strategy for community capacity building, when combined with similar plans developed by other groups.

Methods on how to identify capacity building needs with one community group are described in Resource Four. A group's capacity building plan could include:

- a statement on principles

- a description of learning needs of people involved in the group

- the needs in terms of organisational change for the group

- an outline of costs, funding, timetable and any useful targets.

Key issues in this process are:

- groups may request help to produce such a plan

- the idea of having a plan should not be imposed on the group but arise from its interest in learning and change

- funders will need to consider how to support the preparation of plans

- plans could be drawn up with a network as well as individual groups. Some of the particular needs and features of networks are discussed in Chapter Three.

- it is important to include a statement of principles that will need to reflect and draw on the group's own experience of discrimination and blocks about learning.

For more information on group-based capacity building plans see *Building Community Strengths* (Skinner, 1997).

Planning at neighbourhood level

This section focuses on the planning of community capacity building in neighbourhoods. There are many different approaches in use across Britain; here we describe four approaches as examples. These are based on:

● local action planning

● community groups

● activities and events

● resources.

In practice all four can be used in combination and will help to build a broad approach. While the focus here is on neighbourhoods, many of these methods could be adapted to be useful with communities of interest.

Local action planning

Local action planning involves people in improving the quality of life in their neighbourhoods. Through consultation and involvement methods, it can draw people together to identity what's needed in their neighbourhood and create a neighbourhood action plan. It may involve residents, front-line service-based workers, service managers, ward councillors and voluntary and community groups. Local action plans can take various forms and could include:

● a long-term vision for the area

● a description of what people like and do not like about their area

● a description of services, the environment and facilities

● an assessment of local needs in terms of services and facilities

● ideas on how to address gaps and make improvements.

Creating them can be a great opportunity to involve new people and forge new links between residents and agencies. Such plans generated in neighbourhoods can be combined to inform planning on a district basis, for example, through the community strategy or local area agreement. There is a diversity of forms, including village appraisals, parish plans and neighbourhood action plans in neighbourhood renewal areas. They can lead to actions taken directly by local groups, actions taken by agencies and actions involving both. To be effective the process needs:

● the involvement of all sections of the community

● the backing of key public sector organisations to respond to the proposals in some manner

● a system at district level that can integrate local action plans into the wider planning process

● resources to support these processes that are not short-term.

Organising this in neighbourhoods and villages takes time, commitment and considerable skills. Many neighbourhood renewal areas around the country have developed innovative and effective methods and there is a wealth of experience to draw on.

Local action planning is a useful way to involve people and a focus for building knowledge, skills and confidence. For example:

- as people initially get involved they can be invited to join training or action learning sets

- different stages of developing the plan can lead to different learning needs

- the plan can be used to assess the capacity building needs of the main people involved – this may be a mixture of residents and agency staff

- these learning needs can be integrated into the plan.

EXAMPLE

Neighbourhood action planning in Kendray, South Yorkshire

Kendray is a large estate based on the outskirts of Barnsley. The Kendray Initiative is a neighbourhood management pathfinder partnership funded by central government to improve services in one of the most deprived parts of the country. The partnership is involved in a range of projects in the area as well as working with local service providers. A key element in building local involvement in the Kendray Initiative partnership has been the close working relationship with a long-standing resident group, Kendray Laying the Foundations (LTF). This group meets regularly, and adopts a less formal structure than the Kendray Initiative board, with the meetings being open to all comers. The Laying the Foundations group provides a 'seedbed' for community capacity building, as active individuals are supported by community workers to get involved in a variety of projects and groups, thus developing their skills and confidence. In many cases, over time, people move from being concerned with a single local issue to building a wider view of the needs of the estate and getting involved more in managing local projects. Many LTF members take the further step of getting involved in the board of the partnership itself, which places more demands on people acting as representatives and involved in longer-term planning.

Community groups

A second approach to planning capacity building at neighbourhood level is through focusing on the needs and involvement of community groups. One systematic way to plan support is through what is called a *community strengths profile* – see the box opposite. This focuses particularly on the community and voluntary groups in an area and looks at how they are organised, what their strengths and achievements are, what their aims and needs are, what support they are getting and what support they might need in future. On page 94 we discussed working with one group; the emphasis here is on capacity building planning with a number of groups.

Community strengths profiles have now been carried out in a large number of districts across Britain including Chester, Colchester and Bristol, in Wales and in North Belfast. The method focuses on groups; it does not, for example, specifically look at the needs of individuals as community representatives or volunteers. Community strengths assessments could also be carried out with a community of interest across a whole district or borough such as disability groups. This will be useful for the community of interest to identify its development needs and argue the case for further funding, recognition, and support. Such information, based on a number of communities of interest, could help to inform the development of a district-wide strategy on capacity building.

Assessing community strengths

The approach involves comprehensive local surveys that can provide detailed information leading to recommendations for action. This will be useful for:

- providing a baseline description of the capacity or *strengths* of neighbourhoods and networks

- planning capacity building with support for voluntary and, in particular, community sector groups.

The key feature is that such assessments can provide a systematic description of the baseline of community capacity, by focusing on the needs and strengths of community and voluntary groups. Assessing community strengths includes the following stages and elements.

- **Preparation** – identify groups in the neighbourhood. This may require outreach work to ensure current lists include all groups in the area.

- **A survey of community and voluntary groups** – this asks about how groups are organised, their memberships, aims, plans, training and advice they receive, funding and resources, equal opportunities issues, links with partnerships and networks. This builds up a picture of the *level of community organisation* in the area.

- **A survey of organisations providing support** – this asks about resources, funding, training, information, advice, facilities, equipment and so on that they provide to local community and voluntary groups. This builds up a picture of the *level of support* in the area. It includes the VCS-based infrastructure organisations as well as support based in the public and private sectors.

- **Analysis** – the information gathered from the two surveys is then analysed and draft findings identified.

- **Workshops** – groups and agencies are invited to participate in workshops and open meetings to discuss the draft findings and make recommendations.

- **Plans for action** – these are drawn up, involving voluntary and community groups, local agencies, the local authority and partnerships.

The community strengths assessment would only ever be carried out with the explicit backing of local groups. The questions in the two surveys are divided into the four building blocks, which makes the information more accessible for planning. The findings from the two surveys are combined to identify the key gaps in the area's level of community organisation and level of support. A five-level framework can assist in the interpretation of the findings. These gaps and the recommendations agreed locally can feed into an action plan on capacity building for the area and, if needed, a review of progress can be carried out at a later date. Two key features of the community strengths profile approach are it:

- uses the four blocks to help to collect and interpret the information. Given that the four blocks can act as a guide to planning it is helpful that the profile has been designed with this in mind

- looks at both the level of organisation of groups in the neighbourhood and the level of support.

For further information, see *Assessing Community Strengths* (Skinner and Wilson, 2002).

EXAMPLE

Planning capacity building with community groups in North Belfast

In 2003 the North Belfast Unit, funded by the Office of the First Minister and the Deputy First Minister, carried out an audit of community capacity in North Belfast. This used the *assessing community strengths* approach. The aim was to assess the capacity level of community organisations and the extent of support available. This information was used as a baseline to guide the further planning of resources to develop the capacity of groups. In total 108 interviews were completed, representing a response rate of 63% of the 171 community and church groups identified by the Unit. Almost 60% of the groups indicated that they had not received any outside advice in the previous year regarding the running of the group. Interestingly, it revealed that 42 groups saw themselves as 'cross-community' and 81% of groups had links with other groups to increase understanding between the communities, while 16% of groups had links only with groups from the same community. Fifty-nine per cent of groups indicated that they had been involved jointly with a statutory agency in the previous year.

Activities and events

At local level, organising *activities and events* can create opportunities for involving people in capacity building. Activities and events can, where appropriate, be part of the process of local action planning. For many community practitioners, this is an important way to contact and engage people who may not already be in a group. The capacity building itself may be very informal and not necessarily presented as training or workshops, but can have a key role in developing skills and confidence. Activities and events could be a:

- festival, play scheme or gala
- campaign
- conference or launch
- cultural or arts event
- bus trip or visit
- series of meetings on local issues
- meeting with managers from agencies.

For any one event or activity, there will be different types of skills, knowledge and abilities involved; community workers may help to choose ones partly based on which have the most learning potential. The tasks in any event or activity can be identified – doing this with participants can be part of the learning. People's readiness to get involved and take on certain roles and levels of responsibility will vary over time; someone may start out rather low on confidence, just help in a background way with the play scheme but two years later be running it on a paid basis. On a larger scale, activities and events can be seen as a project that a group organises. In terms of project management, there may be a wider range of tasks and roles which are a source of learning and growth for those involved. The box opposite describes one useful way of defining the stages involved.

The seven stages of developing a community project

A practical tool kit has been developed by the London School of Economics (LSE, 2004) and is designed to help community groups:

● make the process of developing a community project more manageable

● share some common problems

● get ideas and inspiration for where to go for help.

It describes in detail seven stages that are involved in setting up and running a project – what to expect, common problems, ideas and sources of help. The seven stages identified are:

Stage 1 – Agreeing the problem

Stage 2 – Developing a project idea

Stage 3 – Building an effective group

Stage 4 – Writing a plan

Stage 5 – Getting the resources

Stage 6 – Launching and establishing the project

Stage 7 – Where next: measuring, monitoring and improving.

It is a useful way to identify learning for groups embarking on a new project.

EXAMPLE

Planning capacity building around a partnership

One of the approaches used by the Kendray Initiative, based in South Yorkshire, has been consciously to base capacity building around the development needs of its partnership board. The board is well established with 23 members and a spread of residents, community and voluntary sectors' representatives, agencies and ward councillors. Every two years a review is carried out by the partnership's community worker over a two-month period, meeting each board member in turn. This generates information both on individual learning needs and the organisation's areas of development. A report presented to the board acts as the basis of an action plan for capacity building which is carried out over the following period to address the issues raised. The community worker also runs training needs analysis sessions with the board, splitting them into groups of more and less experienced rather than groups based on residents and service providers. This approach has proved to be very effective in involving everyone in helping to build an effective partnership.

Resources

The fourth approach to planning capacity building at neighbourhood level can be through using an existing template of the key resources needed. One such proposed template comes from *Firm Foundations* (Home Office, 2004b). The Firm Foundations report suggests that, for communities, support must be within easy reach within their neighbourhood or parish, or focused on the community of interest with which they identify. The report identifies five key elements to provide this.

- **A hub:** a meeting space or base, which is available, welcoming and accessible to all.

- **Seed-corn funding:** access to seed-corn funding, often small grants, funds or community chest.

- **Community workers:** access to support provided by workers with community development skills.

- **A forum or network:** this needs to be deliberately inclusive, open and participatory, that is owned by and accountable to the community.

- **Learning opportunities:** Access to high quality and appropriate learning opportunities to equip people for active citizenship and engagement.

Consequently, one approach to planning at local level is to carry out an audit to identify to what extent these elements are in place. An action plan can then be drawn up to tackle the gaps in the resource provision.

Working with communities of interest

Across a district there will be many communities of interest that may not easily get involved in neighbourhood-based planning. Based on the experience of some community workers in Bradford, particular principles that can inform practice are:

- support work needs flexibility to recognise what stage people are at in terms of confidence and collective organisation

- where there are common issues, it is useful to bring people together

- sharing experiences in a safe space is important

- it's a slow process and time is needed to build trust and relationships

- it needs skilful community development worker input.

Planning community capacity building at district level

As well as planning that is based in groups or local neighbourhoods, planning for community capacity building needs to be done at a borough, city or district level. We use the term *district* to cover all these in this book. Many of the ten planning elements described earlier will be useful in this context. There are some key additional points.

- At district level, planning will be more strategic than practical. It will need to build on and consider existing policies and strategic plans, such as the community strategy. In addition a compact and a local area agreement can be useful frameworks for strategic planning.

- It will need to ensure key players are involved, such as the local strategic partnership and the local authority, with real involvement of the voluntary and community sectors. In particular, it will need the leading involvement of infrastructure organisations and community empowerment networks.

- Strategic planning at district level can consider the overall picture in terms of *forms of support* available as described in Resource Five. It can also consider the range of *sources of support* for community capacity building as discussed in Chapter Three.

- A strategic approach will need to consider in combination the capacity building needs for agencies, voluntary organisations and community sector groups. The planning model in Diagram 6 above, page 90 will help this process.

- The district may already have a learning plan based on its neighbourhood renewal strategy, and a plan for the development of the community and voluntary sector infrastructure as a part of the Change Up framework. These may need further development to address issues relating to the community sector and community capacity building raised in this book.

Adopting a strategic approach

A strategy developed at district level would provide a framework for the planning work and take a longer-term view. An effective strategy will need to include many of the issues considered above in the planning process but focus more on the overall picture. A strategy on capacity building at district level, for example, would need to include consideration of the following points.

- *The needs and problems* facing both voluntary and community sector groups and organisations, key issues, baseline position and opportunities.

- *The needs and problems* faced by agencies in their community engagement policy and practice.

- *The nature of existing support* both in terms of its *sources* and the main *types* of support available to the voluntary and community sectors. This will include looking at the needs and range of capacity building support provided by *infrastructure* organisations.

- *The policy context* – such as modernising local government, civil renewal, links with appropriate initiatives and strategies such as the community strategy.

- *The stakeholders* – who needs to be involved in implementation, including, for example, public sector managers, service users, council members, representatives of volunteers, local groups, voluntary organisations, communities of interest, community representatives, networks, agencies, service providers and funders, the regional government office.

- *Key aims and objectives* for the strategy. A strategic view could consider a range of development needs of:

  a) *voluntary and community groups and organisations* (described in Chapter Four)

  b) *the infrastructure* organisations (described in Chapter Three)

  c) *support organisations* (described in Chapter Three)

  d) *agencies* in terms of enhanced community engagement (described in Chapter Five).

Ideally, a strategy would include objectives relating to these four aspects of capacity building.

- *A set of principles* that will inform the strategy – these are discussed in Chapter Four.

- *The action plan* – how the objectives will be achieved, description of resources available, and timetable.

● *Feedback* – how practice will be improved and lessons disseminated

● *Evaluation* – how progress will be recorded and assessed – evaluation methods are discussed in Resource Eight.

Building on existing strategic planning

At district level it is useful if all the main voluntary and community sector infrastructure organisations in collaboration with public sector bodies develop a local infrastructure development plan (LIDP). This is a key recommendation of the Government's Change Up strategy and many districts already have one established. Some of these LIDPs have focused mainly on the:

● development of infrastructure organisations

● provision of support to enhance voluntary and community sector-based service delivery.

This is an important base to build on and there is much innovative and thoughtful planning and research invested in these plans. For such a development plan also to address fully community capacity building, they may need to consider:

● the support needs of community groups and active citizens as well as those of voluntary organisations

● support at local, parish, village and neighbourhood level, not just district or sector level

● the development of community anchor organisations

● the needs of networks and communities of interest

● local action planning and related capacity building needs.

Hopefully LIDPs will already be considering these issues, and a lot of creativity has gone into them. In some cases they may need to be broadened in scope to build on the work done so far.

Gathering information for strategic planning

A key issue at district level is, given the scale of the voluntary and community sectors, how can information can be gathered to inform the planning process? In neighbourhoods with a population, for example, of 10,000 people, assessments of the needs of voluntary and community groups can in some cases survey all known groups. At district level this is less likely due to the sheer scale of the voluntary and community sectors. There are various alternatives.

● An assessment of needs can be based on a sample survey of a representative cross-section of community and voluntary groups in the district. In Bradford District, for example, a sample of 70 community and voluntary groups was used, carefully selected to get a good spread of different types of groups, from an estimated total of 3,500.

● Assessing needs and planning can target a particular community of interest. In Bradford District, for example, as part of the neighbourhood renewal strategy, a research project was established specifically to find out about the infrastructure needs of south Asian groups.

● A particular emphasis of a district-wide survey could be to focus mainly on the smaller community sector groups. This may lead to unearthing particular problems and needs being faced by smaller groups that may not be identified in a general sample of voluntary and community sector organisations.

- A fourth option is to carry out assessments of needs in neighbourhoods and over time build up a picture of the whole district. This would mean prioritising certain neighbourhoods in the early stages and having some degree of consistency of approach in order to build up a meaningful picture. Identifying a baseline position of community strengths in different neighbourhoods could be part of a rolling programme of identifying needs (Skinner and Wilson, 2002).

Whatever method is used to gather information, strategic planning of community capacity building will require the ownership of the key players in the district, in terms of the voluntary and community sectors, representative networks, the local authority, local strategic partnership, key agencies and the private sector.

Strategic planning needs to take a long-term view

EXAMPLE

The Stockwell Partnership Community Capacity Plan

This example demonstrates a strategic approach to planning capacity building.

The Stockwell Partnership is the London Borough of Lambeth's community forum. It has used SRB and Urban 11 European funding to support a broad-based capacity plan for the borough which aims to:

- create dynamic, sustainable and confident voluntary and community sectors

- nurture a vibrant civil society

- facilitate the participation of local people in the delivery of regeneration projects.

The plan is based on a range of needs analyses covering local groups. Its activities include:

- training advocacy workers to support minorities accessing services

- setting up a resource library for groups on funding and good practice

- developing forums and networks for underrepresented groups.

Overall the intended outcome is to see greater participation in regeneration and more secure voluntary and community sectors.

EXAMPLE

The Sandwell Partnership strategy for capacity building

This example shows how an over-arching strategy brings together voluntary and community sectors with statutory bodies in a learning programme.

The Sandwell Partnership is the local strategic partnership for the Borough of Sandwell. The Sandwell Partnership board in 2003 approved a broad-based framework, called Working with Communities. The three primary care trusts in the borough took a leading role, with the support of the local authority and other agencies, to work closely with voluntary and community sector networks to produce the framework. The framework includes a statement on values, commitments by different stakeholders, description of roles and methods to engage with communities, as well as the expected outcomes. The implementation plan has combined *building skills* of community leaders with the *professional development* of practitioners by creating eight action learning sets across the borough. These involve people from many different groups and organisations to develop through action learning the skills and knowledge for neighbourhood renewal and community engagement.

Conclusions

In many ways the whole of this book has been a route to this Chapter. The planning of capacity building in broad outline will need to consider:

- the role it can carry out both in terms of the impact on communities and on key policies and services – as explored in Chapter Two.

- the context and needs of the voluntary and community sectors – as described in Chapter Three.

- what community capacity means in practice – based on the four building blocks introduced in Chapter Four.

- how needs and strengths are identified – looked at in Resources Three and Four.

- linking capacity in the community sector to community engagement and the changes needed in large public sector organisations and partnerships – Chapter Five focused on this.

- basing capacity building on a proper consideration of the different ways support can be provided – discussed in Resource Five.

The four building blocks provide a down-to-earth framework for planning and practice that integrates values into the work. In combination with the community engagement model, they help make links between capacity building with communities and in agencies.

We hope that by now you will have some confidence about what all this means and some idea of the practical ways forward. A key thing is don't be overwhelmed – hopefully this book has provided some fairly practical ways in which capacity building can be organised and planned as part of your work on *strengthening communities*.

The Story

Twelve months on and Dave is now well known in the district as a 'community representative'. He walks really slowly nowadays but doesn't care. It's been quite a year. The MS group had organised several visits to disability projects around the city, he'd had a mentor from another group and they had all enjoyed doing the advanced assertiveness course. 'So we are all raring to go now' Jimmy had said. He'd been a bit of a role model for Dave, and Jimmy had passed on his years of experience and good stories. For all the training courses that he had been on, that was the best thing really, thought David, 'long chats over endless coffees, till we all got high on the cigs and caffeine ...'

After six months of negotiation and planning, the MS group had got its first contract with Social Services to provide a range of services across the district. The key thing for the group was that it could now employ paid staff rather than rely on volunteers, and could offer a wider range of support. It was now also organising another protest campaign, this one aimed at a drugs company ...

Gita had turned out to be a really useful contact. After sorting out the contracts with several groups for specific services, she had got a much better idea of what was going on. Her proposals on looking at the development needs of community groups in the city had been approved by the Executive Committee and now had a budget attached to pay for a survey. A major conference organised by a network of groups had brought a lot of people together – and she had ran one of the workshops. The survey was being carried out right across the city with people from disability groups themselves involved in the interviews of other groups.

Gita had done some homework – joining a training course on how voluntary and community groups work, finding out about current government policies on support for groups – something called Change Up and Firm Foundations she'd discovered. Her ideas on having a look at how 'community engagement' was organised in the whole authority had gone down reasonably well with the Director.

'We're all in this together' she had said to Dave one Friday morning and he'd felt quite shocked. They were in her office enjoying a strong coffee. He thought – wasn't this the high and mighty senior manager we had all feared? 'I suppose I've learnt a lot over the last year' she said. 'Your fiery group sort of set the ball rolling.'

And Dave was changing. Getting around as a disability network representative had led him to many new people and places. He had links with new groups and partnerships and enjoyed the ideas and new situations. 'But it needs more' he found himself saying to Gita, 'it needs a combined approach with everybody, not just us, not just the network. That's the next challenge.'

Defining terms

Resource One is a glossary of definitions that can be used in the planning and implementation of capacity building initiatives. Some of the definitions included here are taken directly from existing sources as indicated. In other cases the definitions are ones provided by the author.

A key issue is how to define capacity building. A new definition is given in this publication which replaces an earlier definition given in *Building Community Strengths* published by the Community Development Foundation in 1997. That definition, which was collectively devised by CDF staff, has been used as a key definition of capacity building to date. The new definition offered by the author in this publication reflects current thinking.

Capacity building

> *Capacity building is a process of learning and change that increases the ability of individuals and organisations to contribute to the development of communities.*

Capacity building is an approach to developing abilities and organisational capabilities in any organisation, agency, group, team or project. It is a process of learning and change not focused exclusively on communities, though it has often been used with that emphasis in the past. It is a term already used in organisational development in the public sector.

In this publication we propose that the common underlying feature and aim of capacity building, whether in large agencies or small community groups, is that it leads to the *development of communities*. It can include capacity building directly with and for community groups as well as building the capacity of *infrastructure organisations*, as defined below.

Capacity building can consequently be seen as a general term that can have additional headings attached to it when referring to particular settings, such as *community capacity building* and *agency capacity building*.

Community capacity building

> *Community capacity building is activities, resources and support that strengthen the skills, abilities and confidence of people and community groups to take effective action and leading roles in the development of communities.*

Community capacity building can consequently be seen as one form of capacity building, which particularly focuses on the *community sector* and the participation of people in their neighbourhood or network. (As there is often ambiguity and confusion around community capacity building, we explain each term in the definition in more detail in Resource Two.) This leads to the question of what community capacity itself is.

Community capacity

Community capacity is the ability of people and community groups to work together to take leading and effective roles in the development of communities.

Community capacity is especially about *groups* rather than the larger voluntary sector organisations. The term 'groups' as used here includes both those based in neighbourhoods and those based on shared interest or identity – *communities of interest*. Community capacity is also about *people* and their ability to participate in the development of communities, as leaders, volunteers, activists, representatives and organisers. In this context, it is not about participation or activities focusing on the workplace or within families, or involvement in activities purely for personal gain.

Community strengths

Community strengths means exactly the same as *community capacity* but we prefer to say *strengths* because it is more positive and less patronising. The term *strengths* can be used as an alternative and we hope over time it will come to replace the term capacity.

Agency capacity building

Agency capacity building is learning, resources and organisational change that increases the ability of public sector organisations to engage with communities effectively.

The term *agency* is used here as shorthand to mean a range of public sector bodies, including, for example, local authorities, the police authority, primary care trusts, government offices and departments. In this context, the aim of *agency capacity building* is to improve community engagement, which is explored in some depth in Chapter Five. Capacity building, including organisational development in agencies in its wider sense, can have a range of objectives, often linked to the corporate aims of the organisation, including improving services. In order to focus the discussion in this publication, we limit the discussion of capacity building in agencies specifically to improved practice and policy in community engagement.

Economic capacity building

Consequently capacity building can be seen as a generic process of individual learning and organisational development that can be applied to different sectors. For example, *economic capacity building* is where the intended outcomes are primarily to do with increased wealth and employment. This may mean developing community enterprise, creating environments where economic activity is supported, and developing vocational skills. There is naturally some overlap between community and economic capacity building.

Support

Support refers to practical, organisational, policy and financial help for capacity building for community and voluntary organisations and active individuals. This is how we use the term support in this book – it obviously has many other interpretations and uses.

Sources of support are described in Chapter Three and types of support are discussed in Resource Five.

Community sector

A useful definition of the community sector adopted by CDF is:

The whole range of autonomous collective and group activity, directly undertaken by individuals within their neighbourhood or community of interest, to improve the quality of life.

The community sector is consequently a spectrum, which includes community groups and similar collective activities as a whole. It relates to a range of policies and services, including, for example, activities such as playgroups, tenants' associations, arts and sports groups, environmental and leisure groups, scout groups, religious welfare groups, self-help and support groups, community centres and village halls. The community sector can consequently be seen as the community itself taking action to get things done (Home Office, 2003a).

Voluntary sector

A useful definition is:

'Organisations whose activities are carried out other than for profit but which are not public or local authorities. These organisations would normally be formally constituted and employ paid professional and administrative staff. They may or may not use volunteer help.'

(Home Office, 2004b, p. 40)

The voluntary and community sectors infrastructure

Voluntary and community infrastructure organisations are those based in the voluntary and community sectors (VCS) that play a supporting, representative, policy-making and developmental role for other voluntary and community organisations.

(Adapted from NCVO, 2003)

Communities of interest

The understanding of the voluntary and community sectors has changed in the last few years. Communities of interest are now recognised as a key part of the voluntary and community sectors and can be defined as:

Groups of people who share an identity, for example African Caribbean people, or who share an experience, for example, being homeless, and who often face discrimination and barriers to influencing and accessing services, resources and support.

(Adapted from Building Communities Partnership, 2004)

Explaining community capacity building

In practice, there is often confusion and ambiguity about community capacity building. So Resource Two is a description in some detail of what we do mean – and what we don't mean! To start with the definition used in Resource One:

Community capacity building is activities, resources and support that strengthen the skills, abilities and confidence of people and community groups to take effective action and leading roles in the development of communities

Background to the definition of community capacity building

This definition of community capacity building is based on one developed through the Home Office review of community capacity building, which led to *Building Civil Renewal*, and *Firm Foundations*, both published in 2004. The definition used in those publications was written by the Community Capacity Building Review Team, a working group of representatives from government departments and advisers, including the author, who took a lead role in working on the definition. The team was guided by a broad-based steering group that included a large number of voluntary and community sector networks and organisations. The version given above varies from the Home Office definition only by one word; our version says *development of communities* compared with the narrower focus of the Home Office definition with the wording *development of their communities*.

Each term used in this definition is now explained.

Activities

- *Activities* refers to training and learning opportunities, including a variety of forms of adult learning and informal education, tailored to the needs of members of groups and networks. This means it is not the same as vocational training in community venues, nor is it limited to training as the main form of learning.

- The term *activities* also refers to the organisational development of groups and networks through advice and support, information, facilitation and consultancy.

- Both learning and organisational change can be provided partly through mutual support and sharing between groups – it is not just about learning providers addressing needs.

Resources and support

- *Resources* refers to physical properties such as buildings, assets, office and meeting space, and equipment such phones, copiers, computers and printers.

- It also includes people resources such as childcare for meetings, signers, and interpreters.

- Funding is a key element of *support*; a major concern of groups is its short-term nature.

- *Support* can also include information, advice, guidance, contacts, and administrative assistance where it is useful to community groups and networks. It refers to practical, organisational, policy and financial help.

- It can also include community development support – the provision of paid professional community workers.

So who provides this support? Resources and support can be provided by larger community and voluntary sector organisations as well as from statutory agencies and authorities. In addition, many community groups receive valuable support from each other, through networking and joint working.

Strengthen skills and abilities

- The term *skills* as used here includes knowledge, abilities, talent, empowerment, confidence – it is a shorthand term that means a lot more than just skills.

- It includes the skills of being active in a group, on a local committee or involved as a community representative.

- The term *abilities* used here also applies to community organisations – for many community groups, the process of strengthening also means working on how they are organised.

People

We mean *people* who are contributing, active or involved in their neighbourhood or community in some way – this may be in community groups or involved through informal activities or networks. The term *people* as used in this definition also includes community representatives, mentors, unpaid community workers, volunteers and leaders, members of councils, social entrepreneurs and campaigners. But community capacity building is not about building the capacity of individuals who are involved in local activities purely for their own benefit, or who are unaccountable local leaders.

Community groups

- Community capacity building is primarily about strengthening *community groups*.

- The term *groups* specifically includes both neighbourhood-based groups and communities of interest.

- It also includes formal and informal networks of groups – building well-organised networks can have a major impact on effective partnerships and regeneration programmes.

- Community capacity building provision will often need to involve skilful outreach work to ensure marginalised groups have equal access.

- It will also need to include work within and between groups to challenge discrimination and practices that exclude people.

Effective action

Effective action results in groups more effectively achieving their aims and objectives. Having this as an aim is important because far too often the agenda of capacity building is achieving someone else's aim! Certainly groups will often want to contribute to the aims of the community strategy and other key strategies in a district. In some cases it may mean that by becoming stronger as a group and building capacity, the group says NO! 'We don't want to take on yet more responsibilities and we are happy doing just what we do already and can now do it even better.'

Action in communities is not solely based in groups. *Effective action* in this definition includes practical help between neighbours, in streets and in informal groups. It also includes volunteering, both formal and informal. In combination, it includes all the things that add up to what is often called 'social capital'. Effective action, whether involving individuals or groups, will need to be based on principles of inclusion and equality.

Leading roles

- This refers to contributing to the design and delivery of local services.

- *Leading roles* also means groups and networks having a major impact on policies and management of projects and partnerships.

- Carrying out leading roles will often mean taking initiatives and building assets at community level.

- For people and groups to take on such leading roles, this will often involve large public organisations and agencies changing their systems and procedures to engage with them more effectively.

- This will involve cultural changes in the ways of working in such organisations, and shifts in the power relationships with communities.

The development of communities

This includes a range of social, economic and environmental development, depending on what communities see as their priorities. The development of communities may happen at local neighbourhood level or across a wider area, based on common identity and needs. Community development has been described in a key model called ABCD – which stands for Achieving Better Community Development. It divides community development into a number of dimensions and outcomes (Barr and Hashagen, 2000). An aspect of community development will be building strong communities as discussed in Chapter Two. At district level, the development of communities may be organised through a community strategy and other key strategies around cohesion and participation, where such plans really do reflect people's needs and aspirations.

The Active Citizenship Framework

Active citizenship is a useful concept to bring together a wide range of roles in communities, groups, networks and partnerships. Because of this breadth, it can help to identify needs and strengths of individuals active in their communities. This emphasis on individuals is one approach to identifying needs for community capacity building; identifying the needs of groups is covered in Resource Four.

Active citizenship can be divided into a range of roles that people adopt. These roles in combination can be used as a framework to help planning of capacity building.

● The *Active Citizenship Framework* combines many different types of roles in one list, including social action, volunteering, involvement in public bodies and political representation.

● The Framework will help to identify the range of people and activities involved in the community, their support and training needs, and encourage greater co-ordination.

● Any one person may play a number of roles and their roles may change over time – planning for this is often overlooked.

Active citizenship has a key role to play in any district and what is needed is a common understanding of what is meant by active citizenship that values different cultures, ages and backgrounds. The box opposite gives a description of the types of active citizenship that exist in communities.

The Framework provides a way of looking at the development needs of key people active in the community – be they a good neighbour, member of a group or a magistrate. In terms of scope, the Framework list does not include:

● carers within the family – the assumption is that active citizenship and community involvement starts outside the family

● purely social activity – the Framework assumes, for example, just going to bingo or the pub is not being an active citizen

● purely religious activity – for example, the Framework excludes priests and other religious leaders where the role is primarily spiritual. It does include, however, their roles as channels of communication.

Any one person may have several roles at any one time – helping in their street, fundraising for their group, volunteering in their temple to serve meals and organising a community café, for example. The same person may then over time be elected as a parish councillor or sit on a consultative body on a primary care trust.

The Active Citizenship Framework: Types of active citizens

Voter – votes in parish, district, national or European elections.

Consultee – attends public meetings, consultations, neighbourhood forums; responds to surveys.

Campaigner – individual who reacts to local problems, for example phones the council if the bins are overturned, writes to local newspapers, lobbies for changes in how services are run

Organiser – individual who gets involved in directly organising activities, events, such as neighbourhood action planning, play schemes, local arts events.

Informal volunteer – unpaid help given outside the family, such as practical help for neighbours or occasional help at a local community centre or project.

Formal volunteer – unpaid help organised through a broker organisation such as social services, volunteer bureau or an employer.

Group member – an active participant in a community group, club, faith welfare group, young persons group, or tenants' network.

Group leader – has a responsible position in a community group, club, society, network, such as neighbourhood watch co-ordinator, chair, treasurer, secretary of a community association.

Management committee member – is on a project, community centre or village hall management committee; trustee on a voluntary organisation committee; school governor.

Religious leaders – their role as a channel of communication with and from members of a certain faith but excluding what is primarily their spiritual role.

Social entrepreneur – person who organises social enterprises for the benefit of a community in a paid or unpaid capacity.

Ward councillor – person locally elected onto the district council.

Parish councillor – person locally elected onto a parish council.

Public office holder – such as magistrate or council executive member.

Area-based community representative – person who is elected or selected to be on an area-based partnership such as a regeneration board or sub-group. The role here primarily concerns their area and they are seen as representing it either because they are elected by a local election process or because they can provide local knowledge and a community perspective.

Sector-based community representative – person who is elected or selected onto a public sector consultative/management body such as a primary care trust, university or college management board, policing board or faith network. The role here primarily concerns a particular sector, or part of a sector. They may have been selected by the public agency or selected/elected by a community-based network or user group.

District-based community representative – person selected or elected on to a district-wide strategic partnership, such as a local strategic partnership or other district-wide broad-based partnerships. This may be through a community empowerment network.

How to use the Framework

The Active Citizenship Framework can be used at strategic, district or neighbourhood level to help identify needs and strengths and inform the planning of capacity building support. It could be the basis of research and fact-finding to address questions such as:

- Does the district lack participation in particular types of active citizens? For example, is there is a lack of school governors?

- What capacity building support do different types of active citizens receive? For example, community representatives may need to increase their skills in feeding back information to their own communities.

- Are there particular types of active citizens who need increased support? For example, informal volunteers may suffer from a lack of training and protection.

- Do active citizens move from one role to another? For example, do leaders of community groups become area-based community representatives? Is there progression from less responsible roles to more responsible roles? Is the district losing experienced people who could provide invaluable leadership?

- Are there some general aspects of capacity building common to all types of active citizens? For example, would all active citizens benefit from training programmes on building community cohesion and understanding diversity?

- Are there similarities in training and support needs between different types of active citizenship? Are needs and strengths in other cases different?

If a clear picture could be obtained on these questions, a district would be in a much better position to provide support for its active citizens and in so doing, achieve a better state of governance and participation. It means capacity building could be organised through a systematic approach to developing active citizenship.

How can the Framework be used to plan capacity building support?

- The starting point in using the Framework is to identify what the needs are – and whose. For each type of citizen, a set of questions can be asked regarding their training, induction, ongoing support, reasons for getting involved, reasons for leaving their role etc.

- Identifying support needs can be based in a district-wide partnership that itself has representatives from the different main areas of activity.

- Priorities will need to be drawn up to guide investment in further researching needs. Certain types of citizens may be prioritised for research because of a perceived or known gap in the level of participation.

- Research can involve gathering information from the people involved in the citizen role. It can also be useful to collect information from the organisation the person is based in or working through, such as a community group or agency.

- This may identify some similarities in training and support needs between different types of active citizenship. In other cases, needs may be quite different.

- In some cases the lack of participation may be due to a lack of capacity in the organisation rather than the individual. For example, a community representative may struggle to feel effective on a primary care trust management body but this may be due to the trust's inability to use the representative's contribution effectively.

In using the Framework, the following issues can be considered:

● support for individuals to make best use of and further develop their skills and experience

● increased planning and co-ordination of organisations that support and use active citizens

● opportunities for progression and appropriate support as individuals move between different settings and organisations

● more ways to share good practice between both individuals and support organisations

● further cultural change in large public organisations so that they are geared up for increased community engagement.

There are a number of key principles underlying support for active citizenship:

● All forms of active citizenship are equally valid.

● Active citizens need appropriate support to be able to contribute.

● Support needs to be inclusive of different ages, gender, sexuality, abilities, cultures and communities.

● Public and private sector organisations have key roles to play in effectively engaging active citizens.

● Support for active citizenship needs to build on and value people's existing skills, experience and critical abilities.

● Active citizenship needs to be based on principles of equality and involvement outlined in the four building blocks.

EXAMPLE

The Active Citizenship Framework in use

This example shows how, in Bradford District, the Active Citizenship Framework was used to plan support for community representation.

The Active Citizenship Working Group was made up of people from Bradford Council, the University of Bradford, the Community Network and the local strategic partnerships as well as key voluntary sector infrastructure organisations. The group used the Framework to identify which aspects of active citizenship to focus on for an initial research project. Research was carried out in October 2004 to map current levels of representation in ten key public decision-making bodies across the district. The aim of the research was to find out about practices of these partnerships and agencies regarding recruitment, training and support of community representatives. The research found out that particular problems and gaps were:

● while the participation level of Asian men was good, there were difficulties in recruiting and retaining Asian women

● there was no special provision of support for young people's involvement

● some organisations provided buddying and mentoring schemes

● it was recognised that unrealistic expectations were often placed on community representatives

● most of the organisations would benefit from assistance in developing appropriate governance structures.

The research led to a number of conclusions that the working group then took forward.

Assessing the needs of community representatives

As shown in the Framework, a key area of active citizenship is acting as a community representative. Many community representatives and the networks and organisations that they come from are requesting capacity building so that they can be more effective. Addressing these needs is a particular area of capacity building with a number of key issues to tackle:

- the lack of clarity about the role
- the demands placed on the role
- the environments representatives encounter.

The lack of clarity about the role

A key concern of such individual involvement is about the capacity to be an effective representative. This raises questions about the role of the individual.

- Are they representative because they are seen as typical of some group or type of background?
- Are they representative because they have been elected or selected by a network to which they report back?
- Are they in effect a well-known local person chosen by the public sector body but with little real local accountability?

These questions increasingly worry many community networks, groups and leaders. In some cases, elected members of local authorities question the legitimacy of community representatives. Where appropriate, these issues need to be addressed as a part of community capacity building. There are a number of points that may be helpful to highlight in the process.

- Most academic arguments support the view that such participation can complement elected representation, rather than replace it (Parry et al, 1992).
- Community representatives can be seen in many cases as specifically representing the voluntary and community sectors. This view is put forward by Chanan in *The Practical Effects of Community Involvement* (2004). Where community representatives are selected or elected by a community empowerment network or similar VCS-based network, this is a useful interpretation. Where elected from a local neighbourhood for a local partnership, it would not apply.
- Some community empowerment networks are looking at alternative terms such as *delegate* or *advocate*.

The demands placed on the role

A second issue is more directly related to the individual and the demands put upon them by their role. Some representatives, especially from faith groups, minority groups and communities of interest, are expected to speak on behalf of a whole range of people and concerns within their particular network or community.

The environments representatives encounter

Equally, representatives can face alienating experiences in formal agenda-based meetings, with reams of papers to read (and print!) prior to the meeting – often sent without enough time to consult anyone they are meant to represent.

Many community empowerment networks and VCS organisations are addressing these problems and issues, which directly impact on the capacity building support that people need.

EXAMPLE

Research on community representatives in Leeds

In 2002 Leeds Voice, the voluntary and community sectors network, organised some research into the needs of community representatives. Particular findings were:

● the geographical size of the constituency for representatives made their role almost impossible, given the magnitude of the task

● there were also questions of how such a diverse range of groups and organisations, ranging from local branches of national charities to small groups, could be consulted

● the report recommended training for partners on the role of representatives, their purpose and remit as well as the diversity of the voluntary and community sectors.

The report of the research includes an innovative model describing both the positive and negative 'spirals' of involvement. In the latter, a pattern of lack of acceptance of the role, unaccountable structures and pressures from family life combine with other factors to lead to a downward spiral of frustration and self-doubt. The spirals model helps to identify some of the key factors that affect experiences of representatives and inform capacity building support (Leeds Voice, 2002).

Identifying needs and strengths

Resource Four gives a brief overview of approaches and methods of identifying the main needs and strengths of community groups and their members. Central to this approach is that it is not just about identifying the *needs* that groups and active individuals have. It is also about identifying and recognising their *strengths* – their existing skills, knowledge, experience and talents.

Community capacity building in practice can be about ensuring there are opportunities for these existing abilities to be used and realised, rather than developing anything new. Consequently, in the practical methods described here, there is an emphasis on recognising and starting from the skills and abilities that are present and often underused. This section mostly focuses on community groups – one approach to finding out about the needs of individuals is given in Resource Three in The Active Citizens Framework. So this resource is an overview but not a how-to-do-it guide! More details on practical methods can be obtained in other publications; for further information see the References.

Effective learning and change should be based on a real need for the group and its members. This may sound obvious but it needs to be emphasised. It still happens, for example, that training courses are organised for 'local people' with hardly anyone turning up. Assumptions have been made about what people are interested in, with no real contact with local groups. Equally, a consultant is asked to work with a group to develop its constitution, who then carries out a technical exercise to produce a well-written document, but meanwhile the underlying tensions in the group are ignored.

The ways that people and groups get involved in building their skills and strengths is varied – from casual low-key involvement through just knowing a local community worker, to a need arising from an over-stressed management committee. Some groups may respond to questionnaires and printed publicity or actively seek out assistance; others may need help from a known community worker to encourage them to get involved.

Approaches

Here are four useful approaches to identifying community capacity building needs and strengths with groups. Each approach looks at needs from a different perspective and may influence the choice of method to use.

- *Plans* – the learning needs and existing strengths can be identified in relation to the group's plans and objectives.

- *Problems* – these can prompt a fresh look at the way the group is organised, the skills members have and areas they need to strengthen further.

- *Tasks* – identifying tasks within the activities and roles in the group is a useful approach; it can help to show what the range of tasks is and which areas need further support.

- *Issues* – issues facing the group can be the way in: an issue such as access for different parts of the community to the group and the building it is based in, can be a spur to develop new practices and practical arrangements that in turn require new skills and organisation.

In practice these four approaches can often be combined – an issue may lead to a new plan for the group and the plan can be divided into tasks that will need doing and so on. No doubt the list of four approaches could be extended – it just depends on where the group is at and what approach will unearth the needs and strengths most easily.

Practical methods

We now look at practical ways to identify learning and organisational needs with groups. These can be divided into two categories:

- methods involving direct contact with a single group

- methods involving contact with several groups simultaneously, for example through an area-based survey or open workshop.

In many cases they will involve participative ways of working with the group divided into pairs and smaller groups and so on.

Methods that can be used with one community group

This involves someone with the appropriate skills facilitating the group, using one or several of the following methods. These methods overlap and can be used in combination.

- **Stocktaking** – a method using a set of key questions to help the group review the last year, and from this identify times members struggled with situations and tasks.

- **Future snapshot** – a way of helping the group look ahead to a future desired point, identify activities associated with that point and work backwards to brainstorm the skills, abilities and knowledge required. This could be based on, for example, a general vision of the future for the group or a more specific point in setting up a new project.

- **Project planning** – going through the stages involved in setting up a new project and identifying for each stage what the group will need.

- **Defining tasks** – explores the needs of one person in relation to a set of tasks or role they have in the group, using the equivalent of a job description and person specification.

- **Skills list** – go through a list of skills, abilities and knowledge and ask each group member to identify their strengths and areas of need. Can be usefully combined with the above four methods. The list given in the box below could be a starting point for this.

- **SWOT** – a structured facilitation to explore the four themes of strengths, weaknesses, opportunities and threats which can all help to identify learning and organisational needs.

- **Health checks** – prepared sets of questions that organisations use to identify their organisational strengths and weaknesses, with a rating score for different themes.

Basic principles in identifying needs and strengths

Involve people

It is important in identifying learning and development needs that community groups are involved in the process. If groups feel training and other initiatives are being imposed on them, it may produce negative responses (Cole, 1993). Equally, many groups and members are keen to learn new skills and benefit from the experience; the survey of 25 groups in the Bradford Trident area in 2000, for example, unearthed 15 groups that were interested in getting help to identify their training needs.

Identify strengths

As well as focusing on learning and organisational needs, it is important to recognise the strengths and achievements of groups and networks. This is a more empowering way to work – and it is needed in order to identify gaps. The difference between existing skills and needed skills, for example, would in crude terms inform a capacity building programme.

Recognise fears

Many people involved in community activities have understandable blocks to learning and training. Some people's school experiences may influence their openness to getting involved in anything sounding too structured – people's confidence may need to be built up in stages. Groups also have fears about using outsiders as specialists when they are new to the group, especially where they are being paid hundreds of pounds in a consultancy role!

Challenge exclusion

The very process of identifying needs will itself set the agenda of how capacity building is organised. If you only ask able-bodied people it may well be only able-bodied people who participate! Whose needs? is a key question – which groups or people are chosen to work with and why? In other words, equality and access issues need to be considered from the outset.

Appreciate diversity

Different groups may have different ways of working, based on their background, identity and traditions. People will need the space to work in their own way and may not feel comfortable with new methods brought in that are very unfamiliar.

Have fun

Learning and change does not have to be difficult – it can be enjoyable. Participative, creative methods, chosen with care and that are right for the group's comfort zone, can help make it go with a zing. For groups unfamiliar with learning, a visit to a neighbouring area, for example, organised as a day trip out may be a good way to start.

- **Quality assurance** – systems designed within a national quality assurance framework for the voluntary and community sectors can be used to identify development needs; they may be geared more to larger staffed organisations than to community groups.

- **Policy checklist** – list of policies and practices that organisations need for a specific purpose, for example in order to obtain commissioning funding. Going through the list with a community organisation can help to identify areas of weakness and related training and development needs. Having a quality assurance system in place may be part of the list: see the box opposite.

Many of these practical methods are described with more detail in *Building Community Strengths* (Skinner, 1997).

Eligibility criteria for commissioning

Bradford Council funds and supports a wide range of voluntary and community organisations. In commissioning for services, it needs evidence to show that organisations that are bidding are viable, have appropriate procedures and structures in place and are likely to be able to provide the service they are interested in providing. In order to be eligible the commissioned organisation must be a voluntary or community group with a constitution, and provide:

- a satisfactory management structure

- an equal opportunities policy

- evidence of a bank account

- satisfactory financial procedures

- an annual budget

- last year's accounts

- a complaints procedure

- a health and safety policy

- evidence of having adopted or working towards a recognised quality system

- insurance – public liability and employers

- contracts of employment

- grievance and disciplinary procedure

- job description/s and personnel specifications.

Working with a number of groups

There are other approaches that are useful when involving several groups at once. This may be across a neighbourhood or with a community of interest-based network of groups. Useful methods are:

- **Questionnaire survey** – a set of questions with a covering letter usually circulated through the post or email to the target groups in a district or neighbourhood. Central to a good response is whether the group will perceive any benefit from completing the form and, to some extent, how well it is designed. If the covering letter comes from a well-known VCS organisation or network, it will usually increase the response rate. Email circulation is being increasingly used for surveys, though there are questions about whether this narrows the respondents to those who can afford to be online.

- **Open workshops** – informal open meetings that bring together people from a large number of groups. Can be combined with other methods, be good on networking and fun, and help to build confidence. Some workshops use focus group methods.

- **Telephone survey** – contacting groups by phone has the distinct advantage of less leg work. However, some groups may not respond well to phone-based enquiries, even with prior contact through a covering letter. There are limits to the number of questions that can be reasonably covered in a telephone call, which may limit the range of information gathered.

- **Conference** – can be combined with all of the above methods to bring people together. This can be to gather information or just present findings in order to invite discussion and build some ownership of the process.

These methods mean more groups can be contacted in a short period than methods that involve only one group at a time. However, the response rate can be a problem and without further support and follow up, it may be that less organised and excluded groups are the ones who have a lower level of response.

EXAMPLE

Research into groups' needs in Bradford District

Longitudinal research was commissioned by the Building Communities Partnership to look at the support and development needs of the District's voluntary and community groups.

Called 'Res.com', the research was carried out between March and May 2004 with 70 voluntary and community groups. The sample included newly emerging groups, established small groups, groups employing one to two employees and larger voluntary organisations. The sampling technique also ensured samples of a diverse range of groups were included: for example black and minority ethnic, disability, lesbian and gay, older people, and women's groups and groups from different types of neighbourhoods district-wide. All the 70 groups were visited by a researcher who facilitated group discussions around a range of organisational development issues. The format of the discussion encouraged groups particularly to consider issues they had faced within the previous 12 months. The range of areas considered included groups having their say, organisational issues faced by the group and the type of support they could benefit from. The focus group discussions were all transcribed and placed within NVIVO software to enable analysis. Res.com can be used as a data resource for exploring a range of issues related to active citizenship. Most obviously it can provide evidence of the support needs of voluntary and community groups in getting new members and developing them.

Using specialists

Identifying the development needs of a community organisation can be quite complex. For this reason many groups will invite someone from outside the group to help. Specialists have a role to play here. The development work may involve a range of activities and practical methods. These can be divided into four main roles:

- **facilitation work** – for example, to clarify roles, resolve tensions or plan the future

- **research** – to gather new information or interpret existing data

- **advice and information** – for example on the type of legal structure needed to start a new project

- **analysis** – to give a view of the cause and nature of the problem and propose a way forward.

EXAMPLE

Action research on capacity building needs

This example demonstrates a workshop-based approach to identifying needs. In North Bradford a regeneration partnership, Regen 2000, commissioned action research on capacity building needs of women in its area. The approach used reflected community development principles. It involved:

● interviewing 20 key workers from agencies about provision, priorities and targets

● organising a consultation event – inviting agencies and groups together to look at current provision, gaps and priorities (42 people from 30 groups attended)

● a draft report with recommendations which were then fed back to a workshop to consider the details of the recommendations – 18 people from 10 organisations attended

● producing a final report with an action plan.

An outcome of this research was the establishment of a local network – and the spin-off is working together in partnership that will build community capacity.

There may well be no clear dividing line between identifying the development needs and actually resolving them – in some cases all an outside specialist will do is define the problem and suggest ways forward – the actual changes in the organisation may happen later, or even not at all! The classic mistake when using a consultant is to see the final report as the outcome rather than just a stage in the changes needed.

Using stakeholders

The methods described so far involve working directly with the group or several groups. Other sources of information are:

● existing reports and surveys

● background papers and strategies

● stakeholders.

We examine the third source further. There may be some benefit in some cases from also involving people who already know the groups in question, and asking them for their perception of development and learning needs. These could be:

● local community workers

● funding organisations

● infrastructure and support organisations

● local projects and centres

● council officers involved in community development

● trainers and specialists.

These people can be called *stakeholders*. They can bring useful information and perspectives that add to those gained directly from the group. Equally they may bring biased and partial information. There are two key issues to consider.

● is such consultation with stakeholders carried out with prior approval of the group?
To do so would be likely to lead to a loss of trust

● is the information gained confidential and if so, how useful is it?

Stakeholders can have a useful role to play but consulting them needs some careful consideration if it is to be used effectively.

EXAMPLE

Appreciative Inquiry: Brisbane Creative Communities projects

Appreciative Inquiry is an approach to capacity building that focuses on the strengths of a community, enhancing the positive and building on what is already working well. The Appreciative Inquiry Framework within a community setting has been developed by people such as Sue Hammond and Joe Hall www.thinbook.com Appreciative Inquiry also draws from therapeutic and organisational development disciplines where work focuses on the historical strengths of an individual/family or agency. Appreciative Inquiry focuses on searching for solutions rather than defining problems, and amplifying what works rather than what does not.

In Brisbane City Council in Queensland, Australia, community planning and urban design strategies have incorporated Appreciative Inquiry into a number of projects. The Banyo Library, based in an indigenous (aboriginal) area, started to explore its community using a positive inquiry approach. Using a film crew, they asked the first person to come through the door a number of questions. These were on what people liked about their area, what they think it did well, who else they knew, and what they liked about them. This included asking for an introduction to the people they knew and led to repeating the questions with them, thus building a series of enquiries.

These questions, along with other questions, developed a mass of positive data, within a documentary film format, about the built environment, positive values and meaning of a place and people's involvement with their community. The film and other materials were then shown as part of an outdoor event with a high level of local interest. This event in itself created significant positive energy for community leaders and agencies to work with. Strengths were further analysed, connections made and projects developed, including the development of computer clubs with local indigenous people and redesign of streetscapes, community facilities and local parks.

Supporting community capacity building

Resource Five looks at a range of ways that funders, larger voluntary and community organisations, public sector organisations and partnerships can support community capacity building. This needs to be organised in a planned manner, in combination with other partner organisations and, in particular, voluntary and community sector organisations that provide infrastructure support.

Here we give an overview of the range of ways that support for community capacity building can be provided. Each possibility is described briefly in order to give a wide range of ideas rather than a lot of detail. In combination, based on local needs and priorities, they can be used as part of a planned approach.

Chapter Three included a short description of the range of organisations that can potentially provide *sources* of support for community capacity building (pages 32ff above). This Resource focuses on the *type* of support rather than the *source*. Essential to this work is that it starts in and belongs to communities. What we need to avoid is a hotch-potch of individual schemes and funding streams, organised in a top-down manner, with little grass-roots ownership or wider co-ordination.

In addition to the types of support described here, an important issue to consider is *community development work*. This is described in Resource Six. Community development work often needs to underlie the use of the options described in this Resource for them to be fully effective.

So here we give short descriptions of a range of ways to support community capacity building. This Resource describes a menu of options that could be examined in relation to needs and strengths. These options for support will need to be considered in planning capacity building, both at local level and more strategically across a whole district. These planning issues are looked at in Chapter Six.

Ways to provide support for community capacity building

Develop a database of community and voluntary groups

A key aspect of developing the strengths of groups is to know how many there are, where they are based, what they do and who they do it for. Usually in any one district or neighbourhood there exists a number of lists of information on groups; these may be based in the infrastructure organisations, such as a council for voluntary service, rural community council or additionally in the local authority. Often such lists have been compiled separately over time. Creating an up-to-date database of all community groups and voluntary organisations that lists basic information is a very useful tool to use to find out more about their support needs. Many community empowerment networks have developed databases of member groups and often act as a network of networks. Gathering such information strengthens the planning process and is often a crucial first step.

Support the identification of community capacity building needs

Many groups are keen to receive help with identifying their needs and strengths. This obviously needs to be organised in ways that are accessible and participative. Providing funding and staff resources that directly address the identification of learning and organisational development needs of groups can be a very useful input into the provision of community capacity building. Issues involved in this were discussed in Resource Four. Such work is partly about recognising and using the existing skills, experience, organisation and achievements of groups. Any such initiatives need to be linked to the likely future availability of capacity building support, so that identifying needs and strengths leads to some direct follow-up work. A framework for finding out about the needs of active citizens is given in Resource Three.

Mapping the level and range of support

The planning of support needs to consider the existing pattern of support and its various sources in order to address gaps and challenge inequalities. It would be useful to start with a baseline picture of the level of support and the way it is organised.

Consequently, a good starting point at neighbourhood level would be to identify who those organisations are that can or could provide such support, and survey them to collect information on the range of support they provide. This approach has been tried and tested at neighbourhood level in many parts of Britain using the community profile method called *Assessing Community Strengths* (Skinner and Wilson, 2002).

Fund research into the support needs of particular groups

Funding such research could target resources for under-represented and excluded groups and communities of interest to find out what their capacity building and on-going support needs are. In Bradford District, for example, the Joseph Rowntree Foundation has funded research to find out the needs for infrastructure support for the South Asian communities. Such initiatives are a way of then using the research to inform funding decisions on capacity building infrastructure and community development support.

Provide practical resources

Research has shown some of the practical resource needs community groups and networks have (Purcell and Brown, 1995). Providing practical resources is much more effective when it is based on an audit of what is already available and what is needed. Effectiveness is also increased when the availability of resources is described in a resource guide, either in printed form or website-based – and preferably both.

Provide technical services

Technical services can be, for example, free or subsidised professional advice from surveyors, architects, accountants, solicitors, public relations and IT specialists and managers. Such schemes need to be advertised and set up with clearly defined roles for participants and beneficiaries. Providing technical services can be very useful to groups but needs to be organised in a planned way, within a framework of partnership between organisations, rather than as an ad-hoc charitable venture.

Providing capacity building support to community and voluntary groups

What do we mean by *support?* Here are some examples of support for community capacity building using the four building block headings (see page 4):

Support that helps to build community organisations

- Access to rooms and halls for meetings; access to office space and equipment; free or cheap office furniture; practical assistance with administration; access to low-cost auditors; access to funding information.

- Access to computers with word processing, spreadsheet, database and desktop publishing programs; access to the internet, laser printers; printing equipment; photocopier; fax and franking machines; presentation materials and display boards; overhead projectors, flip chart paper and video equipment.

- Advice on team work and business planning; information on funding sources and making bids; legal information; professional advice from architects and auditors; information on constitutions and financial planning, guidance on partnerships and legal structures; advice on employing staff; secretarial assistance.

Support that helps to build involvement

- Employing community development staff who help new community groups to get established and develop their structures and organisation, who can provide practical support and administration for groups and networks.

- Providing help for groups to find out about local needs and work jointly with other groups and agencies.

Support that helps to build skills, knowledge and confidence

Organise or directly provide training courses designed for members of voluntary and community groups; books and videos on managing projects; grants and child care to help people involved in groups access training courses; information on how the council works; mentoring schemes for members of community groups; practical help with groups to organise visits to other centres and projects as a learning opportunity; resource library on capacity building and community development.

Support that helps to build equality

- Providing training on cultural awareness for community groups; help writing equal opportunities policies and action plans; running campaigns.

- Providing information on equal opportunities issues and relevant legislation.

- Providing guidelines on recruitment and selection procedures; access to translators and signers; grant aid to make buildings accessible; provision of equipment such as portable hearing loops; access to Braille production; space, staff and equipment for crèches for meetings, events and courses.

Source: *Assessing Community Strengths* (Skinner and Wilson, 2002)

EXAMPLES FROM THE PRIVATE SECTOR

There are a number of ways in which companies can support capacity building for community groups and networks. Some companies provide these services free or at subsidised rates for local groups:

- arrange access to company in-house services such as printing and design
- offer access to meeting rooms and training facilities
- give access to in-house training courses
- provide technical and legal advice
- provide an accountancy service for local groups
- grant aid and gifts in kind
- staff time as volunteers and on secondments.

Often companies prefer to build a relationship with a neighbourhood or group rather than engage in just a one-off project.

Employ staff for community capacity building

Staff can be employed by an organisation to work in and with communities to build community strengths. They will need clearly defined job descriptions, supervision from managers who understand the issues, and liaison with other similar practitioners. Central to the personnel specification of such practitioners are community development skills; these are defined in the Occupational Standards on Community Work – see Resource Six. Too often staff members have been appointed without such skills and supervision, and in some cases carried out poor quality work which is too loosely called capacity building.

Organise specialist assistance

In addition to in-house technical support and capacity building, workers, independent consultants and trainers can provide community sector groups and networks with a wide range of advice, facilitation, training, research and evaluation. Public and private sector organisations can support increased access to such specialists in a number of ways, described in the box opposite.

A key issue is that specialists working with groups have the appropriate skills and experience of community settings and issues.

We paid good money for a funding adviser who
raised nothing and taught us nothing

Directly fund community capacity building activities

Public and private sector organisations can directly fund community capacity building activities and provision. This can be organised through a distinct capacity building funding pot or as an aspect of a broader fund for VCS activity and services. Either way, funding can be directed to a

How specialist assistance can be provided

- Organise and maintain a directory of specialists, listing freelance trainers, advisers and consultants.

- Establish a central fund to grant aid organisations wishing to engage specialists on a paid, short-term basis.

- Establish a community chest fund that can be used quickly to provide groups with small amounts of money for help with preparing briefs and tenders. This would be prior to engaging a specialist but may itself require paid help, for example, for two days.

- Where providing grant aid, cater for paying for specialist help within mainstream revenue funding to community organisations.

- Fund infrastructure organisations to provide a service of organisational development assistance to community groups.

- As an agency, directly employ specialists who can offer assistance to groups.

- As an agency, develop a training programme for potential specialists including experienced members of community organisations.

- Establish a pool of specialists who are chosen specifically to work with community groups.

Support at local level

Firm Foundations recommends key components for support at local parish, village or neighbourhood level:

A hub: A meeting space or base which is available, welcoming and accessible to all. This could be a physical hub such as a community centre or village hall, school, community flat or shop, or development trust or settlement, or a virtual hub such as a website or e-mail network.

Seed-corn funding: Access to seed-corn funding, often small grants, funds or community chests, which have proven very cost-effective in stimulating grass-roots activity and capacity building.

Community workers: access to support provided by workers with community development skills, within the framework of values that underpin community development.

A forum or network: this needs to be deliberately inclusive, open and participatory, that is, owned by and accountable to the community. This could be, for example, a network of community groups, a broad-based community association, a tenant management organisation or a neighbourhood partnership.

Learning opportunities: Access to high quality and appropriate learning opportunities to equip people for active citizenship and engagement. These will range from formal courses, through mentoring to informal sharing of ideas and experiences. All must be grounded in people's own experiences, and be seen to have direct practical value.

wide range of capacity building activities and programmes or limited to a particular type of need or issue – such as developing equal opportunities policy and practice – or for a particular type of group – such as disability groups. In terms of mainstream grants and commissioning funding, a proportion of the funds available for projects and services in the VCS could be dedicated to learning and organisational development.

Directly fund infrastructure organisations

As a part of the Change Up strategy, many areas have developed a clearer picture of their infrastructure needs, in particular because the early spend resources available in 2004 were often used for mapping and assessment exercises. A key issue here is how such funding provision for infrastructure and the direct funding of capacity building activities originating from public sector organisations relates to other funding available in a district for capacity building; there is a need for co-ordination between partners within a broad-based strategy on capacity building, integrating both Change Up and Firm Foundations as frameworks for planned support. Essential to such initiatives is that the voluntary and community sectors take a lead role.

Fund support work with communities of interest

This may mean skilful outreach work to get to know and involve excluded and minority groups. Many such groups, by definition, may not be organised into networks or federations and the support offered should not assume one size fits all. Building strengths in this context will need flexibility and adequate resources, allowing time for relationships to develop, both within communities of interest and with larger organisations.

Directly fund community anchor organisations

As described earlier on page 35, these are particular types of VCS organisations that specialise in community capacity building at neighbourhood or village level. The idea is promoted in the Firm Foundations report. Funders from the public, private and voluntary sectors can invest in *community anchor organisations* to enable them to become more sustainable. This can take the form of what is called 'patient capital' where the terms are soft and over a substantial time period. The Adventure Capital Fund is an example of such a scheme that offers a combination of business development grants, working capital and low interest loans, coupled with tailor-made organisational development support (Thake, 2004). Also as a part of Firm Foundations, central government is supporting the appropriate transfer of assets to community anchor organisations. This involves encouraging the consistent application of the rules for such transfers and building management capacity in anchor organisations.

Support the development of community representation

As described in Chapter Five, effective community representation is a key aspect of community engagement. Public sector organisations can support the development of skills and systems for such participation by directly funding specific training programmes and working at district level to identify support needs. This will involve working jointly with community networks and leaders to ensure such initiatives are grounded in the VCS. An approach to this, called the *Active Citizens Framework* is described in Resource Three.

Community development work

Community development work involves a range of methods and skills, solidly based in a strong and explicit value base. Using and employing community development workers when organising capacity building can substantially increase effectiveness. There is the strong advantage that experienced community development workers have the practical know-how of working in and with communities.

This can include skills and knowledge such as:

- understanding the dynamics and tensions in communities

- how to develop organisations

- practical support and sharing skills in organising events and activities

- working with both groups and networks

- support to build confidence in individuals

- working at the interface of communities and the pubic sector.

In particular regarding the last point, community development workers can play a key role as brokers, building relationships between community groups and agencies.

Overall there is a case for properly-resourced community work provision to complement the main capacity building initiatives; effective community work at neighbourhood and network level can be seen as the essential preparation and on-going support to any capacity building programmes. Across Britain there is a spread of community development workers based both in statutory agencies and in the voluntary and community sectors. A recent trend has been local authorities commissioning their community development function to the voluntary and community sectors.

What roles are involved?

The national occupational standards outline clearly the skills, values and practice principles required for community development work. They consist of six key roles that workers adopt, and they outline the skills needed to carry out these roles. The standards are very useful when designing jobs involving community development, planning training in community development skills, and evaluating practice. The six key roles are:

- develop working relationships with communities and larger organisations, including partnerships, agencies and local authorities

- encourage people to work with and learn from each other
- work with people in communities to plan change and take collective action
- work with people in communities to develop and use frameworks for evaluation
- help community organisations to reflect and develop their own practice and roles.

What's the purpose?

According to the national standards, the key purpose of community development work is:

'Collectively to bring about social change and justice by working with communities, those defined geographically and or those defined by interest to:

- *Identify their needs, opportunities, rights and responsibilities*
- *Plan, organise and take action*
- *Evaluate the effectiveness and impact of the action.*

All in ways which challenge oppression and tackle inequalities.'

The standards are available from the Federation for Community Development Learning at www.fdcl.org.uk

What are the likely outcomes?

Characteristic outcomes of community development work are:

- a higher level of social capital
- a better networked, more varied, accessible and inclusive community sector
- more effective community groups
- greater motivation and confidence in active citizens
- more joint working between groups and public agencies.

(Adapted from *Firm Foundations*, Home Office, 2004b)

These are in parallel with the outcomes of community capacity building which are described in Chapter Two. Two useful publications on community development work are:

- *Building Practitioners' Strengths* (Wilson and Wilde, 2001)
- *Community Work* (Twelvetrees, 2002).

Community development work in relation to community capacity building

What particular contribution do community development workers make in the specific context of capacity building and the community and voluntary sector's infrastructure? This can be defined as to:

- enable the setting up of new groups
- give groups on-going support
- assist in building participative structures
- ensure equality of involvement
- develop voluntary community work involvement.

These are now explored in turn.

Enable the setting up of new groups

The establishment of new community groups, perhaps prioritising parts of the neighbourhood or community in general where collective involvement is low, is a key aspect of community development work. This type of grass-roots neighbourhood work is essential to avoid the pitfall of agencies responding mainly to already established and more articulate groups.

Give groups on-going support

Community capacity building, as well as involving the development of skills, concerns personal development, individual change and increased confidence. To be effective, these processes need not only be associated with specific inputs of training programmes or time-limited assistance involved in organisational development. Community workers – whose skills especially lie in the area of personal empowerment – have an essential role to play in providing on-going support in the areas of personal confidence and empowerment.

Assist in building participative structures

The building of participative structures and the skills of organisations involved in them – both community groups and public sector organisations – takes time and is itself a developmental process. Meaningful participation requires preparatory work in potential target areas prior to the capacity building process.

Ensure equality of involvement

Outreach work may be needed to build relationships with excluded and marginalised groups, such as some communities of interest, to ensure their views are being heard on how capacity building provision could be adapted to their needs and to encourage participation. Such relationship-building work requires cultural sensitivity and the growth of trust, and may need a specialist additional community work input.

Develop voluntary community work involvement

Many paid community workers adopt an important role of supporting the skill development of unpaid community workers – locally-based organisers and campaigners who have a valuable resource of skills and experience to offer their own areas. This resource can itself make a significant contribution to community life and is in need of support both to recognise and develop it. Community workers, apart from acting as role models in some respects, can help to steer people towards learning programmes and accredited courses on community work.

Community engagement information sources

This Resource describes useful publications and information sources on the theme of effective community engagement.

- The ODPM Beacon Council status scheme 2005 *Getting Closer to Communities*, where selected local authorities disseminate information on their practices to other councils, provides a wealth of ideas and good practice available across the country. For information access the ODPM website: www.odpm.gov.uk

- *Public Policy in the Community* by Marilyn Taylor, published by Palgrave in 2003, gives an excellent overview of participation issues. In policy terms, there is a long and complex history in the UK to the conceptual basis of community participation that reflects a variety of ideological and political positions.

- The Department for Education and Skills is developing a range of performance indicators to measure the level of voluntary and community sector engagement in Connexions. For further information access the DfES website: www.dfes.gov.uk

- The Scottish Centre for Community Development has produced a very useable set of benchmarks for community engagement, called the National Standards for Community Engagement. For more information see the Centre's website: www.sccd.org.uk

- *Community Involvement in Health* by Smithies and Webster (1998) contains very useful material on organisational development, including a model on community development and organisational change.

- *Managing Organisational Change* by Paul Tarplett and Laurie McMahon from The Office for Public Management (1999) is a useful work book for those interested in the management of change.

- The Local Government Association published guidelines jointly with the Compact Working Group in 2000 to help to develop local compacts. For further information see www.thecompact.org.uk

- The Cabinet Office has a guide to engagement called *Viewfinder: A policy-maker's guide to public involvement* published on www.cmps.gov.uk/policyhub

- The Neighbourhood Renewal Unit has a useful website on sharing good practice www.renewal.net.

- The Federation for Community Development Learning has information on Good Practice Standards in Community Development Work. Contact them at info@fcdl.org.uk

- 'The Public Engagement Toolkit' produced by the NHS Executive, Northern and Yorkshire is available at www.doh.gov.uk/nyor/toolkit.htm

- *The Guide to Effective Participation* by David Wilcox (1994) is a useful model of levels of participation. It is available at www.partnerships.org.uk/guide/index.htm

Evaluating community capacity building

This section looks at how community capacity building can be measured and evaluated. It gives a broad overview of the issues involved, describing a range of approaches, and refers you to sources and practical guidelines. In many ways, evaluating community capacity building is subject to the same issues and problems as any evaluation process in the social and public policy arena. However, there are specific issues to consider. The aim here is to give you a brief outline of what to consider and help you to design an effective evaluation. Please note that the evaluation and measurement of community capacity building as a field is still in its early stages of development.

Why carry out evaluations of community capacity building?
This can be in order to:

- improve practice and learn from the experience
- identify if resources were used well
- find out the impact on individuals and groups
- find out the impact on a neighbourhood
- find out the impact on the voluntary and community sectors
- find out the impact on services and quality of life in a district.

We will consequently need to know about:

- the inputs used
- the processes used
- the outputs in terms of what it produced
- outcomes in terms of the impact of the capacity building.

Bear in mind there is a key difference between *monitoring*, which involves collecting and analysing information, and *evaluation*, which is a more thorough process involving assessing effectiveness against stated objectives. Evaluation consequently involves interpretation and judgement.

Another important concept is that of *indicators*. These are single, measurable facts which can be about input, output or outcomes. Outcome indicators can be part of an evaluation or used on their own. They are likely to give you the simplest headline-style facts and figures about your results, and so should enable you to answer the hard questions which funders, users and the public often ask. However, indicators have to be simplified down to single, unambiguous factual statements, and therefore they do not explain the context or process, which will need to be done by a fuller evaluation.

Consider what level you are evaluating

Who or what will be the focus of the evaluation? This will depend very much on the nature of the capacity building and who was involved. Here are some options:

- **Individuals** – such as volunteers, individual members of groups, local leaders, campaigners, and community entrepreneurs. This may involve prioritising particular groups, such as women or people with disabilities.

- **Groups and projects** – such as a residents' or user group, community association, project or locally-run community centre.

- **Programmes** – community capacity building for effective implementation of a government programme at local level.

- **Workforce** – staff and managers in community and voluntary organisations.

- **Networks** – a large number of groups or individual members.

- **Neighbourhood** – addressing the needs of a large number of local groups and geographically-based communities.

- **Communities of interest** – where people share a common identity or experience.

The level at which you are evaluating and monitoring will inform the type of questions you are addressing. Here are some examples.

- **Individuals** – do they show increased skills, abilities and confidence, for example, to take part, organise, manage, work collectively, be enterprising, resolve conflicts, represent, contribute to decision-making and act on the basis of equality?

- **Community groups and networks** – do they show increased abilities to involve people, provide formal services, provide informal services and act on the basis of equality?

- **Neighbourhoods** – does the area show an increased level of community strength?

These three examples derive directly from the definition of community capacity building given earlier in Chapter Two. As you can see, each part of the definition is addressed.

Community capacity building means activities, resources and support that strengthen the skills, abilities and confidence of people and community groups to take effective action and leading roles in the development of communities.

How

Evaluation can involve collecting two main types of information:

- **hard information** – facts and figures: in other words, *quantitative*

- **soft information** – perceptions, views, attitudes: in other words, *qualitative*.

There is not, however, a clear dividing line. Soft information can be made 'harder' by putting it into a quantitative form, for example through a survey of the number of people who agree with a certain statement about their perception of being empowered. Both forms of information can be collected through a variety of methods including, for example, interviews, questionnaires, observation, focus groups and case studies.

The information will need to be collected in relation to a set of defined objectives that the evaluation will focus on. These will need to be clarified before any information collection work is started or monitoring system is established. You will need to look carefully at your objectives. A central issue is: have you got adequate ways of judging whether you are achieving your objectives? This should be a key priority for effective evaluations.

The evaluation process itself can contribute to the capacity building activities. It may be an opportunity to develop skills and for a group to review its form of organisation.

When

● **Start early** – A classic mistake is to wait until the end of a capacity building project and then attempt an evaluation. Evaluation needs to be built in at the start of the project in order to define the objectives, set up an information collection system if needed and, in some cases, identify the starting point – that is, a baseline position.

● **Mid-way** – a review of progress at a half-way or mid-way point can be useful. It can help to bring out issues that need addressing in the second half of the work. In some cases funding bids will need to be produced before the end of the capacity building programme, and a mid-way review may become all the more useful.

● **End of the activity** – this could be the end of a course, project or programme or when a specialist has completed their support work with a group. A key question now is whether the impact of capacity building is to be seen some time *after* the end of the activity, when changes can be seen in terms of the use of new skills or the operation of a new structure in the group.

Whenever you start, it is important to look at any relevant recent evaluations or monitoring or if there are indicators already in use. These may well influence your approach.

Key issues

There are several key problems associated with evaluations in this context, some of which are of a general nature and some of which are more specific to community capacity building.

The difference between output and outcome

Evaluation is often confused with what is purely a monitoring exercise. *Output* targets are usually presented in terms of hard information called indicators, such as the number of participants on a training course or number of groups assisted with organisational development. Such information, however, does not tell you very much about the impact that the training or support actually had on the group. It is also useful to collect information on the actual impact of the outputs: the *outcomes*. These can often also be defined as hard data in the form of indicators.

The level of outcome

One issue is whether the evaluation is of the progress of groups or of wider changes in a neighbourhood. For example, over a two-year period, 20 groups in a neighbourhood participate in training (output) to improve the effectiveness of their groups (objective). An evaluation may evaluate the impact of the training on the groups. It may demonstrate, for example, that five participating groups obtained new funding and set up new projects. This is one level of outcome – the impact the training had on the groups. A second level of outcome could be the impact these groups, now being better organised, has on the neighbourhood or on the regeneration partnership's programme. The outcome therefore depends on the initial objective – the overall aim of the capacity building activities.

The complexity of assessing the causes of changes

Assessing the wider impact of capacity building is a more powerful and informative process than just monitoring outputs. However, the problem can be in actually identifying the causes of changes that are observed. For the example under the previous heading, if five groups did obtain new funding, was it because of the impact of the training – or would it have happened anyway? In the complex environment of social change, a variety of causes may be present. One way of dealing with this dilemma is to use case studies as a part of the process of collecting information. A detailed look at several groups in our training example may unearth what actual difference the training made to how the groups operate, identify the process of change and establish to what extent the training made a difference. A second approach is to combine evidence from several different sources, such as from the participating groups as well as other key stakeholders in the area.

The resource implications

Collecting information on both outputs and outcomes (including making use of case studies and, if appropriate, a variety of sources), has cost implications. There is the question of who carries out the evaluation, either internally or using an external specialist. The design of the evaluation will need to consider the resources available. Using residents as community researchers can have the benefit of developing skills and employing local people but may itself require considerable amounts of support, and should not be assumed to be a cheaper method.

Using outcome indicators

Sets of outcome-based indicators to measure community involvement are now available – see box opposite. These can be used to:

- establish a baseline on community involvement in an area or district

- set targets for improvement

- assess if progress has been made.

To collect data, information would be gathered from local residents, voluntary and community organisations and public service providers.

Such indicators certainly have their role to play. They can help:

- community workers present factual information on the effects of their activities

- service providers to identify benefits from community involvement more clearly

- LSPs and neighbourhood renewal programmes to measure progress in community involvement.

A similar approach could be adopted to measure progress in community capacity building. However, the use of such sets of indicators needs to be used bearing in mind the following points.

● They often assume more is better. But, for example, if an area has 50 more community groups after five years, is that necessarily a better state of affairs?

● By definition, using outcome indicators in a whole neighbourhood or district is to choose a limited number for which data can be gathered relatively easily. These may not always be the most useful indicators, and used in isolation may not be an adequate information base to plan support for capacity building.

● In promoting the use of such indicators by LSPs, local authorities and agencies, it would be useful if guidelines were produced that presented the indicators as one tool in the context of a wider range of methods.

Using outcome indicators

Sets of outcome-based indicators are now available that measure community involvement. Examples are:

● percentage of residents who feel they can influence what goes on in their neighbourhood

● percentage of residents who have been helped by others (unpaid and not relatives) three times or more over the last year

● percentage of residents who feel that their local area is a place where people from different backgrounds can get on well together

● percentage of community groups aware of sources of help to organise more effectively.

See *The Practical Effects of Community Involvement* (Chanan, 2004) and *The Library of Local Performance Indicators: Community Involvement Indicators* (Audit Commission and IDeA, 2002).

The Learning, Evaluation and Planning (LEAP) approach to evaluating capacity building

LEAP is a framework to help pose critical questions about community development and capacity building, and is useful for funders, policy-makers, practitioners, and community and voluntary groups. The framework provides five clearly laid out steps for the planning and evaluation process, using both output and outcome indicators. It also includes a look at the processes involved in capacity building in terms of, for example, training, network development, building confidence or group work. It integrates planning with evaluation with direct cross-referencing of questions to aid the process of collecting information. LEAP is based on ABCD (Barr and Hashagen, 2000) and is now used widely in Scotland.

Useful publications on evaluation

Six useful frameworks for evaluation and benchmarking are described here. Some can be used for capacity building; others are more generally about community participation, but may be able to be adapted.

Achieving Better Community Development (ABCD)

Originally a framework for understanding, planning and evaluating community development and capacity building produced for the Department of Health and Social Security in Northern Ireland. It was subsequently rolled out through a series of training courses across the UK and further developed into what is now ABCD. The Community Development Foundation (CDF) now takes the lead in providing ABCD training courses and publications in England and Wales. ABCD was developed further in Scotland into the LEAP method which is described in the box above. Publications and training courses on ABCD and the full LEAP handbook are available from the Community Development Foundation. See www.cdf.org.uk

Active Partners

A set of 12 benchmarks, key considerations and indicators of community participation in regeneration. Active Partners was commissioned by Yorkshire Forward and developed by COGS with the help of people living in regeneration communities in Yorkshire, including communities from coalfield communities in Wakefield and the Dearne Valley, in 1999–2000. The benchmarks provide a framework to inform the development and review of community participation strategies. They were initially designed for use by Single Regeneration Budget partnerships but are now used in a wider range of settings including neighbourhood renewal programmes and health initiatives. To find out more, access the Yorkshire Forward website www.yorkshire-forward.com

Assessing Community Strengths

A practical handbook for planning capacity building, based upon adaptation of the ABCD framework described above. It provides detailed guidelines for carrying out a 'community strengths' survey, a subsequent assessment process to find out about the strengths and needs of community organisations and the agencies that support them, and action steps for a development strategy. The survey and assessment process was developed and piloted in a New Deal for Communities area in Bradford in 2000. Financial support from the Joseph Rowntree Foundation enabled Steve Skinner (formerly Bradford Council) and Mandy Wilson (COGS) to write up their work. *Assessing Community Strengths* was published by CDF (2002) and is available from them. See www.cdf.org.uk

Auditing Community Participation

A handbook of checklists and appraisal exercises for assessing the level of community involvement and participation in regeneration partnerships. It was written by Danny Burns and Marilyn Taylor and published by Policy Press on behalf of the Joseph Rowntree Foundation in 2000.

Local Performance Community Involvement Indicators

A set of indicators for community involvement developed by the Audit Commission in 2001–02 following consultation with a range of organisations from the voluntary and community sectors, academia and local and central government. This set of indicators is included in the library of the Improvement and Development Agency (IDeA). It is intended that local authorities and other public sector agencies, local strategic partnerships and community and voluntary organisations will use the indicators. See *The Library of Local Performance Indicators: Community Involvement Indicators* (Audit Commission and IDeA, 2002).

Measures of Community

A study of how measures can be applied to judge whether communities are flourishing, based mostly on local authority size areas. It looks at individual activity, community involvement, services and economic activity, issues of inclusion and diversity and infrastructure support. The emphasis overall is on the extent and quality of community life. *Measures of Community* was written for the Active Community Unit of the Home Office by Gabriel Chanan of CDF in July 2002 and is available from them. See www.cdf.org.uk

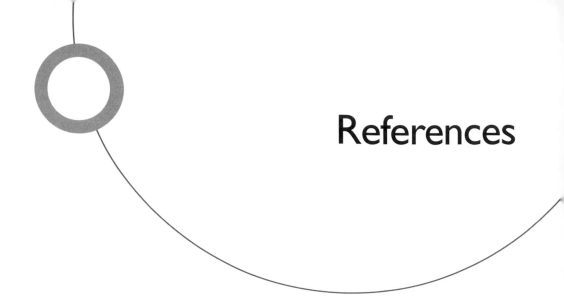

References

Publications

These include both publications referred to in the text and other useful material for further reading.

Arnstein, S. (1971) 'Eight Rungs on the Ladder of Citizen Participation' in Cahn, E.S. and Passett, B.A (eds) *Citizen Participation Effecting Community Change* New York: Praeger Publishers

Audit Commission and IDeA (2002) 'The Library of Local Performance Indicators: Community Involvement Indicators' London: Audit Commission and IDeA

Barnard, H. and Walker, P. (1994) *Strategies for Success: A self-help guide to strategic planning for voluntary organisations* London: National Council for Voluntary Organisations (NCVO)

Barr, A. and Hashagen, S. (2000) *ABCD Handbook: A framework for evaluating community development* London: Community Development Foundation

Barton, P. (2003) *Community Capacity Building and Voluntary Sector Infrastructure in Rural England* London: DEFRA

Birch, D. (2002) *Public Participation in Local Government: A survey of local authorities* London: ODPM

Blunkett, D. (2003) *Active Citizens, Strong Communities* London: Home Office

Building Communities Partnership (2004) *The Building Communities Strategy 2004–09* Bradford: Building Communities Partnership

Burns, D. and Taylor, M. (2000) *Auditing Community Participation* Bristol: Policy Press

Burns, D., Heywood, F., Wilde, P. and Wilson, M. (2004) *What Works in Assessing Community Participation?* Bristol: Policy Press

Cantle, T. (2001) *Community Cohesion: A report of the independent review team* London: Home Office

Centre for Voluntary Action Research Aston Business School (2004) *A Summary of the Active Community Unit's Pilot Studies of Governance Support for Small Voluntary and Community Organisations* London: Home Office

Chanan, G. (2002) *Measures of Community* London: Community Development Foundation

Chanan, G. (2004) *The Practical Effects of Community Involvement* London: ODPM

Chanan,G., West, A., Garratt, C. and Humm, J. (1999) *Regeneration and Sustainable Communities* London: Community Development Foundation

Chandler, D. (2001) 'Active Citizens and the Therapeutic State: The role of democratic participation in local government reform' in *Policy and Politics* vol. 29 no. 1

Civil Renewal Unit (2004) *Active Learning Active Citizenship* London: Home Office

COGS (2000) *Active Partners: Benchmarking community participation in regeneration* Leeds: Yorkshire Forward

Cole, G.A. (1993) *Personnel Management* London: DP Publications

Community Work Training Company (2005) *The Yellow Brick Road* Bradford: Community Work Training Company

Cooke, S. (2003) *Voluntary Sector Infrastructure: A discussion paper* London: NCVO

The Countryside Agency (2003) *Quality of Life in Tomorrow's Countryside: Implementing the Countryside Agency's strategy* Cheltenham: The Countryside Agency

Denham, J. (2001) *Building Cohesive Communities: A report to the ministerial group on public order and community cohesion* London: Home Office

Department for Environment, Food and Rural Affairs (2003) *Community Capacity Building and the Voluntary Sector Infrastructure in Rural England* London: DEFRA

Department for Environment, Food and Rural Affairs (2004) *An Evaluation of Community Engagement in Achieving Sustainable Development in England* London: DEFRA

Drake, K. and Mitchell, L. (2005) *Does Size Really Matter?* London: NCVO

Eade, D. (1997) *Capacity Building: An approach to people-centred development* Oxford: Oxfam

Eade, D. and Williams, B. (1995) *The Oxfam Handbook of Development and Relief: Volume 1* Oxford: Oxfam

Ellis, A., Hindley, A., Macmillan, R., Scott, D. and Servante, D. (2004) *No Overall Control: Experiencing community development in rural Britain* Manchester: The Centre for Applied Social Research, The University of Manchester

Federation for Community Development Learning (2001) *The National Occupation Standards in Community Development Work* Sheffield: FCDL

Field, J. (2003) *Evaluating Community Projects* Leicester: National Institute of Adult Continuing Education

Gaventa, J. (2004) *Representation, Community Leadership and Participation: Citizen involvement in neighbourhood renewal and local governance* Brighton: Institute of Development Studies. The report is available on: http://www.ids.ac.uk/logolink/initiatives/info/NeighbourhoodRenewal.htm

Gilchrist, A. (2004) *Community Cohesion and Community Development: Bridges or Barricades?* London: Community Development Foundation

Gilchrist, A. (2006) *Community Development and Networking* London: Community Development Foundation

HM Treasury (2002) *The Role of the Voluntary and Community Sector in Service Delivery* London: HM Treasury

HM Treasury (2005) *Exploring the Role of the Third Sector in Public Service Delivery and Reform* London: HM Treasury, DTI and Home Office

Home Office (2001) *Active Communities* London: Home Office

Home Office (2003a) *Guidelines on Community Engagement* (internal document) London: Home Office

Home Office (2003b) *The Compact Code of Good Practice on Community Groups* London: The Home Office

Home Office (2004a) *Building Civil Renewal: Government support for community capacity building and proposals for change* London: Home Office

Home Office (2004b) *Firm Foundations* London: Home Office

Home Office (2004c) *Change Up* London: Home Office

Home Office (2004d) *The Benefits of Community Engagement* London: Home Office

Home Office (2004e) *What Works in Community Involvement in Area-Based Initiatives?* London: Home Office Online Report 53/04

Hope, P. (1992) *Making the Best Use of Consultants*, Framework in Print

Hyatt, J. (1995) *Calling in the Specialists* London: Community Development Foundation

Learning and Skills Council (2004a) *Working Together* London: Learning and Skills Council

Learning and Skills Council (2004b) *Learning for Active Citizenship and Community Development* London: Learning and Skills Council

Leeds Voice (2002) *Listening to Community Representatives* Leeds: Leeds Voice

Local Government Association (2004) *Community Cohesion – an action guide* London: LGA

Lloyd, P. (1996) *Social and Economic Inclusion through Regional Development Luxembourg*: Office for Official Publications of the European Commission

LSE (2004) *The Seven Stages of Developing a Neighbourhood Project* London: London School of Economics

Mullins, L. (1993) *Management and Organisational Behaviour*, London: Pitman

National Audit Office (2004) *Getting Citizens Involved: Community participation in neighbourhood renewal* London: National Audit Office

NCVO (2003) *Voluntary Sector Infrastructure* London: NCVO

NCVO (2004) *Almanac* London: NCVO

NCVO (2005) *Does Size Really Matter? Collaborative working between large and small voluntary and community organisations: a scoping study* London: NCVO

Neighbourhood Renewal Unit (2003) *Single Community Programme Guidance* London: Office of the Deputy Prime Minister

ODPM (2002) *The Learning Curve* London: Office of the Deputy Prime Minister

ODPM (2003a) *Single Community Programme Guidance* London: Office of the Deputy Prime Minister

ODPM (2003b) *Sustainable Communities: Building for the future* London: Office of the Deputy Prime Minister

ODPM (2004a) *The Future of Local Government* London: Office of the Deputy Prime Minister

ODPM (2004b) *Local Area Agreements: Advice note one* London: Office of the Deputy Prime Minister

ODPM (2004c) *Local Area Agreements: A prospectus* London: Office of the Deputy Prime Minister

ODPM (2005a) *Why Neighbourhoods Matter* London: Office of the Deputy Prime Minister

ODPM (2005b) *Vibrant Local Leadership* London: Office of the Deputy Prime Minister

ODPM and Home Office (2004) *The Safer and Stronger Communities Fund Implementation Guidance* London: Office of the Deputy Prime Minister and Home Office

Parry, G., Moyser, G. and Day, N. (1992) *Political Participation and Democracy in Britain* Cambridge: Cambridge University Press

Prudue, D., Razzaque, K., Hambleton, R., Stewart, M., Huxham, C. and Vangen, S. (2000) *Community Leadership in Area Regeneration* Bristol: Policy Press

Purcell, R. and Brown, S. (1995) *New Directions – a summary of an enquiry into community organisations in Scotland* Glasgow: The Scottish Community Development Centre

Rogers, Ben and Robinson, Emily (2004) *The Benefits of Community Engagement – a review of the evidence* London: Active Citizenship Centre

Rogers, R. (1990) *Managing Consultancy* London: NCVO

Skinner, S. (1997) *Building Community Strengths: A resource book on capacity building* London: Community Development Foundation

Skinner, S. and Wilson, M. (2002) *Assessing Community Strengths: A practical handbook for planning capacity building* London: Community Development Foundation

Smithies, J. and Webster G. (1998) *Community Involvement in Health* Aldershot: Arena

Tarplett, Paul and McMahon, Laurie (1999) *Managing Organisational Change* London: The Office for Public Management

Taylor, M. (2003) *Public Policy in the Community* Basingstoke: Palgrave Macmillan

Thake, S. (2004) *Sustainable Futures: Investing in community based organisations* London: New Economics Foundation

Twelvetrees, A. (2002) *Community Work* Basingstoke: Palgrave Macmillan

Whiteley, P. (2004) *Civic Renewal and Participation in Britain* Colchester: University of Essex

Wilcox. D. (1994) *The Guide to Effective Participation* Brighton: Partnership

Wilson, M. and Wilde, P. (2001) *Building Practitioners' Strengths* London: Community Development Foundation

Woodward, V. (2004) *Active Learning Active Citizenship* London: Home Office

WYLDA (2004) *Meeting the Needs of the Community and Voluntary Sector in West Yorkshire* West Yorkshire Local Development Agencies

Contacts

- For more information on Bradford District's approach to neighbourhood renewal, contact Bradford Vision on 01274 43 5480.

- For more information on work with communities of interest in Bradford District contact the Communities of Interest Working Group, CNet, Bradford on 01274 71 4144.

- For a copy of *Working with Communities* telephone the Sandwell Partnership on 0121 500 1470.

- For more information on peer learning in the West Midlands, contact Daniel Morris, LSP Regional Support Coordinator by email: danielm@rawm.co.uk

- For more information on the example of capacity building in Brisbane, Australia email Peter Browning: Peter.Browning@slq.qld.gov.au

- For access to Change Up, see the website: http://www.homeoffice.gov.uk/comrace/active/developing/index.html

- For information on DEFRA's capacity building initiatives, see the website: http://www.defra.gov.uk/rural/voluntary/default.htm

- For a copy of the *Seven Stages of Developing a Neighbourhood Project*, go to www.lse.ac.uk/LSEHousing

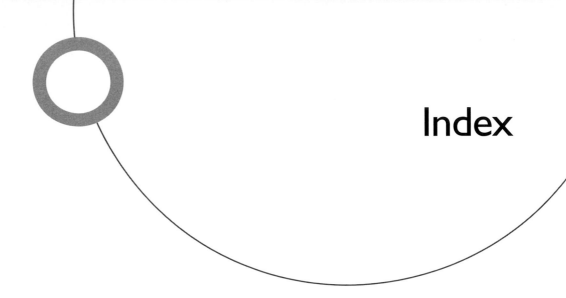

Index